Coming to Terms with Historical Trauma

A Memoir

Sara Pol-Lim

Coming to Terms with Historical Trauma

A Memoir

Sara Pol-Lim, Ed.D.

Table of Contents

Dedications

In Loving Memory of

My father, Vantha Pol, 40 years old in 1976

My brother, Varen Pol, 9 years old in 1976

My brother, Baron Pol, 8 years old in 1977

My youngest brother, Phirum Pol, 6 years old in 1976

My maternal grandfather, Ros Sok, 62 years old in 1976

My paternal grandfather, Juenn Pol, 71 years old in 1977

My paternal grandmother, Vanna Pol, 68 years old in 1977

My father's brother, Van Vanthorn Pol, 28 years old in 1977

My father's brother, Vanjeun Pol, 25 years old in 1977

My father's brother, Vannarith Pol, 23 years old in 1977

and other extended relatives whose mom's accounted for sixty-five people.

To the millions of people who perished during the Khmer Rouge regime: May you rest in peace, knowing that your anguish will not go unheard.

I am also dedicating this book to my maternal grandmother, Mak Yay, who inspired me to keep on learning. Yay Sambok Ven and Saveoun Ven.

Prologue

As humans, we have become experts at focusing on our differences. We have been brainwashed to focus on the things about us that are unique and unusual and not the same. Despite my horrific past, I strive every day to believe that we humans have more in common than less.

Reflecting on my past, I am grateful for the Cambodian people. Kindness, compassion, generosity, and respect for all living things are the natural characteristics of my people. I smile when I think of Mak Yay, my maternal grandmother, who embodied the definition of being Cambodian through my eyes. I was fortunate to have the opportunity to reunite with her before she passed away in the state. Theravada Buddhism was deeply ingrained in Mak Yay and many of the Cambodian elders I encountered. Buddhist practices surrounded their culture and values. I was taught to respect elders, teachers, and authorities. I was taught to do charitable deeds to achieve enlightenment in the next life.

I saw Mak Yay practicing kindness daily, sharing her food with neighbors who had less than she did. She treated everyone with respect, no matter what their status in life is. I often laughed because she gave insects the same respect she gave to people. When flies landed on our food, she gently shooed them away, waving her hand over the meal as if in a friendly gesture.

"There is no need to kill," she protested as I raised my hand to smack the tiny insect. I had full intention of harming the daring creature for being audacious and feasting on our food before we could enjoy it.

Love and generosity are what we practiced as a family. We would give it to others before giving it to ourselves. It was what Mak Yay was taught. It was what Mom and Dad did, as I witnessed them taking in distant relatives to live with us in the city so that they could go to school. Both of my parents worked to support five children and a household. We did not seem to have the best of everything, but we seemed to have enough for satisfaction.

I assumed that every household exemplified the same level of generosity and affection as my own. Sadly, that was not the case. Fear gripped the city as the children went missing, and my parents warned us never to wander off alone for fear of abduction. I also remember the siren warning us to take shelter from possible explosions. I remember being shoved into an underground bunker more times than I could count. However, my parents did not explain why. We carried on living as though nothing out of the ordinary had happened. Looking back, I wondered how it was possible. How was a functioning democratic society sharing no news of what to expect? Wasn't there already TV? After all, it was 1975. There was no warning. There was no preparation.

I can remember no political discussion in my household. I did not see any concern in the expression of the adults, including my parents. How was it possible that they failed to plan? There was a civil war going on besides the almost decade of war nearby in Vietnam. If children are the future, shouldn't there be a plan to protect them primarily? Was there a task force set up to find the missing children? For sure, there was an effort made to ensure the safety of those missing children. It appears that society expected kindness and compassion among Cambodian people to be intact. There would be no harm to children because we were good people to begin with. Trust in humanity was at an all-time high.

However, as of April 17, 1975, I learned that the Cambodian people had a dark side. Those very people I assumed were gentle, and kind killed millions of their own, including children. How am I supposed to judge the Cambodian people now? How am I supposed to live with myself after witnessing such cruelty? It was during the Khmer Rouge regime that I was overwhelmed by hatred and the absence of kindness, compassion, and conscience. The experience left me asking: What happened to the culture and religion that promoted the respect of human life? What drove people to believe that the end could justify the means?

All of it happened when I was only nine years old. I could feel myself emotionally carrying the burden of a mature adult who had lived a hard life. I was just a little girl who enjoyed playing freely in the park. Suddenly, I found myself as a young girl working for the state and observing the events that occurred during Cambodia's turbulent period in history, where Cambodians were in conflict with each other. The torment of watching my three brothers die, one by one, was unbearable. It stained my heart with inhumane images.

The gentle and kind people who resembled Mak Yay became the untrustworthy individual in my heart. They became my perpetrators. How can I ever view them differently after nearly four years of misery I was put through? I lived in fear in those years. Every day, I expected it to be my last day on earth. It was not enough to use me as child labor, but to strip me of having any freedom, rights, and a basic need such as proper nutrition to survive was the ultimate sanguinity. I was placed in multiple children's camps for all those years. I never understood why, each season, the children's camps were disbursed. I would start a new camp in a new location. Looking back, it was a consolidation of whatever was left to the child labor force. Children seemed to be vanishing in the dark of night. I saw less punishment during the day except for minor crimes of stealing food out of hunger or being unable to perform duties as assigned when the body could no longer function.

I did not understand the patriotic lesson to be productive for the government, yet the intensity was to work each kid to death without proper nutrition and care. I remember learning the political rhetoric of "children are the future." How contradictory was it? What the Khmer Rouge preached and how they behaved were completely different.

Instead of filling our young minds with hopes and dreams through literature, books, and beautiful languages, we were told to be dumb, to ask no questions, to do what we were told, to have no possessions, even our families. We had nowhere to belong except to the invisible Angka (government) who forced us to work with the bare minimum of nutrition.

Suddenly, I became ignorant of everything around me. I saw no evil and heard no evil. Perhaps that is the reason I survived. Meanwhile, my mother kept count, recording the loss of sixty family members during the Khmer Rouge regime. I often wondered why I was spared. Having surpassed the statistical probabilities of surviving past my teenage years, I valued my life and did not take it for granted. At the same time, I struggled to find meaning in life. I chose jobs supporting others to justify the gratitude that I was given a second chance to live.

After years of being deprived of food, I wanted so much just to indulge myself with food. Food was my primary motivator to live and to do well in life. Yet, I knew that it was not all about me. It was about the people who did not make it alive, especially the children, my three brothers. How could I not talk about their existence and their last moment in life? How could I let them down by not remembering how they fought to stay alive through starvation, overworking, and unsuccessful diseases? If I failed to remember them, I would be a disgrace to their spirits or whatever force that allowed me to escape the odds of death.

Therefore, I knew my purpose was to find out what had happened through the lens of a nine-year-old girl. I will not allow my father and brothers to die in vain. They, too, needed an answer to why they were the sacrificial humans to the senseless revolution.

Besides, I owe it to myself to find the truth about what happened. I want to know what I did wrong to face such persecution during the Khmer Rouge regime. I hope by knowing what has happened, I can come to terms with my historical trauma.

Now that I am a parent, I have more reason to understand the past. I want to ensure that my worldview is one of optimism and clarity, not skepticism and despair. It is important to have no unresolved grief so that I can live a healthier lifestyle. Even though grief has no expiration date, at least I have a coping mechanism to handle grief when it appears with no warning sign.

This book is written in memory of the innocent individuals who perished under the Khmer Rouge regime, with particular acknowledgment to my father and three brothers. I also hope to promote healing among Cambodian communities in the United States and around the world. By understanding our historical trauma, we might achieve reconciliation within groups and families with different points of view.

This book reveals my past and my experience overcoming my own historical trauma. Through education, I was able to accept and understand the genocide era in Cambodia and find my life's purpose through helping others discover theirs.

Chapter One
An Ordinary Family

Mak Yay-(grandmother) Lavorn Ven Ros

Mom & Me (1994)
We wore the dresses she made

Aunt Fany arrived in America in 1975 with some keepsakes, including this family photo. I happened to be taken with her family and younger uncles. I was the girl in a ponytail. To my right was my brother Varen, who perished during the Khmer Rouge. Left: paternal grandparents, Pol Juenn and Pol Vanna.

Below is a picture of my father in 1975.

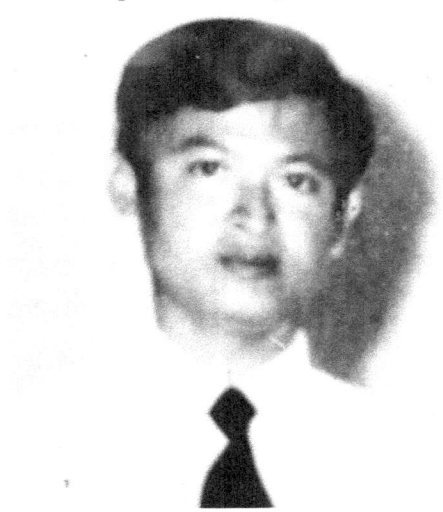

My family was as ordinary as any family. Even though we lived in the city of Phnom Penh, where we were born, we worked hard. My four siblings and I were children. Our job was to go to school every day. Perhaps this fact made us different from the children who lived in rural areas.

We lived in an apartment building near a large single home on the block. The single home belonged to Dad's cousin and his family. What I remembered about the apartment was the rooftop where we dried our laundry in one section. The laundry lines were in rows. It was good for playing hide-and-seek. The other part of the rooftop was an outdoor patio. I recalled a time when we picnicked on the roof with bamboo mats and pillows to gaze up at the stars and watch the full moon or even the eclipse. It was a simple life in the city.

On the other hand, the backyard was small. There was a bunker in the backyard. Occasionally, my brothers and I were shuffled inside the bunker until our parents told us to come out. I had no idea why, but the experience seemed

3

painless. I could not recall the number of floors in the apartment, but my mother confirmed that it has only one floor. I did remember the simple design of the inside of the apartment. It was just a straight rectangular shape without any innovation. There was a hallway where I could see through to the front door and the street. The interior was divided into three sections. The back had the kitchen and bathroom, while the bedrooms in the middle were divided by curtains. The front served as the living room, dining area, and our playroom, offering a clear view of the street. A front gate covered with flowering vines served as a natural fence. There were small pots of herbs surrounding the front entrance. We walked along the concrete sidewalk to school each morning. The best part about our small apartment was the house next door, where I often went over to play with other little girls. In addition, we would get tutoring after school from the young aunt there.

Dad and Mom worked full-time. We had Yay Reun (grandmother Reun). She was our live-in-housekeeper and Nanny. Mom said she was an extended relative needing a job and a place to live in the city. In addition, there was Bong Yorn, the extended relative from the countryside that Mom took in. He was in his teenage years. He frequently accompanied us to school. After a few years, he moved back to the countryside. Since then, no one had heard from him.

Being the only girl among five children I enjoyed the extra attention. However, I was the second child. Therefore, I was expected to set a good example for the younger siblings. Nonetheless, we were only a year apart in age, except for the youngest boy. Mom had all of us when she was in her early twenties.

On the other hand, Dad was older than Mom by five years. He was part of a family with seven children, including six boys and one girl. He was the oldest. His parents adopted a girl to complete the needs of a daughter. In Cambodian society and culture during that time, it was necessary to have at least one girl. The girl was expected to be the caregiver of aging parents. Of course, this might not be the case for my parents. Regardless, Dad was proud to have a girl. Mom went overboard with her hobby as a seamstress. She crafted numerous floral dresses for me to wear.

Whether I happened to complete the gender gap of being their children, I never felt neglected. I could always see the beaming expression on my father's face, as though he enjoyed being a family man. He looked satisfied with life. It was like a dream come true for him. At the same time, he never wanted to miss a chance to shine with his parents. It was his accomplishment to produce a girl when they could not. Dad's humor made him very likeable.

Somehow, being the only girl was not lonely. I was able to play with my brothers. For some reason, I had a vivid memory of playing with my brother, Virak, which led to me falling off a tall stool backwards and hitting my head on the tile floor. I did not recall how old I was then.

It was mentioned that I had a high fever for a few days. After I recovered from the illness, I was not able to stand up, let alone walk. Panicking, Mom, and Dad took me to see a specialist right away. The thought of me becoming crippled was devastating to them. Fortunately, they had access to Western medicine. In Phnom Penh, only French hospitals were considered the best and available at a price, of course. They took me to one of them. I remember being strapped for head stimulation every day. Mom said it took weeks before I showed any sign of improvement. I also had to do physical therapy. Mom said I was about five years old at the time. Mom confirmed that I had Polio. If it were for the treatment, my condition would be severe. Gradually, I was able to regain my mobility and was back to normal.

Mom and Dad were ecstatic. They knew that they were blessed. Polio was an unknown disease for those who did not understand Western medicine. There was no vaccination available in Cambodia. I wondered how many children were disabled by Polio. I had no idea how lucky I was. One thing I remember when I enjoyed going over to my grandmother's house to play was because of a girl named Srey Keo. She lived in a detached room. Her parents rented the downstairs room while they were working in the city. Srey Keo often stayed home by herself. She was older and taller than I was at the time. She was gentle, soft-spoken. The only misfortune was that she could not walk. However, she was proficient at using her bottom as a scooter. Her legs were straight. She could not even bend her knees. However, she moved quickly using her hands and butt. She was incredible. I would climb up and play with her for hours. I was told she had been disabled since she was a toddler. I realized I could have been in the same situation if my parents had not acted quickly to get help. At the same time, my parents believed in the progress of Western medicine, whereas Srey Keos' parents accepted the condition as fate.

They brushed it off as her karmic debt from the last life. It was their Buddhist interpretation. Regardless, I would visit Srey Keo every chance I got. I climbed a few steps into her living room, where she usually stayed. The wooden floor was slippery and shiny because Srey Keo navigated life on it every day. When it was a hot day, the wooden floor was cold. I liked lying there and sharing whatever new toys I got. It was comfortable. Somehow, I felt connected to Srey Keo.

Although, I could not imagine being Srey Keo. She was kept indoor because of her handicap. She was alone most of the time I saw her. She never saw the outside world or the outside playground period. Yet, she never complained about her challenge. She accepted her fate. She appeared friendly, kind, and cheerful whenever I saw her. Perhaps I remember her because of her optimism and human spirit. It took me a while to ask Mom about Srey Keo.

"Whatever happened to Srey Keo and her family that used to live in the downstairs rooms at Mak Yay's house," I asked. Mom did her research when she was looking for her siblings.

"I heard she died with the entire family." I stayed quiet. Somehow, it was not surprising to me. Apparently, they were all killed during the evacuation period. Without an appropriate wheelchair, Srey Keo couldn't leave. Her parents refused to leave without her. As a result, they were victims of the Khmer Rouge's cruel policy.

I was furious at the lack of compassion. What made those young soldiers of the Khmer Rouge to be such contemptible? They were told to clear out the city of human existence. They were told to kill if anyone failed to obey. They did their jobs without conscience or compassion? It was like they were not from the same human species, let alone the same fellows whose were born and raised in the same country. Moreover, when I learned that hospitals had to evacuate and sick patients were left to die, I was numb.

I was more traumatized. The children were not the exception. The most vulnerable population was not considered. In my mind I began to question the values of what we were raised with. My three younger brothers had no chance to live when human kindness disappeared.

My older brother, Virak, is the lucky one. He escaped the Khmer Rouge with Mak Yay, aunts, and uncles to the United States in 1975. It was because of high-ranking military families in the naval base that they were able to escape through months at sea. Just because they avoided being killed under the Khmer Rouge, it did not mean that they were free from displacement due to war. It was not easy for Virak to be all alone in a new country without the comfort of their parents and siblings. He often worried about us being stuck in the Khmer Rouge. It was after eight years that he was able to reunite with Mom and me. By then, he spoke mostly English. I spoke mostly Khmer. It took us a long time to have good conversations between the two languages.

My brother Virak acts strong. But, deep down, he is gentle and compassionate. He joined the U.S. Army right after High school. It was the only way feasible for refugee families with limited resources. When we were children in Cambodia, I remember Virak being terrified of ghosts. It was almost common knowledge in the family. Perhaps because our younger uncles used to scare him with ghost stories. He could not use the bathroom without shutting the door, and my other brother loved to tease him by turning off the light while he was inside. The moment the room went dark, Virak would scream and dash out, never finishing what he was doing. Somehow, growing up in America since he was ten, he was able to overcome every shortcoming as he dared to join the U.S. Army with multiple deployment duties. Dad would be so proud of his accomplishments.

My second brother, Varen, was only eight years old in 1975. He was most likely to succeed. He was self-assured. He knew what he wanted in life at such an early age. He was destined to make significant contributions to the medical field. He developed the habit of maintaining cleanliness, which was uncommon among us. He was unusually clean and meticulous. His utensils had to be washed in hot water. He stored them separately from us to avoid any contamination. After each meal, he would wash his own utensils and put them away. He did the same with all his possessions. Organization was his top priority. He was the only child who would make his own bed regularly. I assumed in today's world; we considered him OCD (obsessive-compulsive disorder). Perfection was his endeavor. As for me, perfection was not always attainable, but perseverance got me through challenges.

My third brother, Baron, was six years old in 1975. He was exceptional, in my view. In some way, it was inherent in his nature to safeguard those who were vulnerable. At a young age, he made it known to the family that he would enlist in the military to serve and protect. His bravery and courage shined. Perhaps he was surrounded by uncles in the Navy. He displayed such stamina and resilience when he visited Aunt Fany and her husband, the commander in the Cambodia Royal Navy, at the base in Riem prior to the Khmer Rouge. He met officers and high-ranking officials without being timid of his intention to be at their level when he grew up. He had a profound influence on numerous individuals. When my mother and I encountered some former officers, they inquired about Baron. Reluctantly, Mom would say he died during the Khmer Rouge. Then, the conversation ended, and the room became quiet. The adults feared to continue further when the words Khmer Rouge were mentioned. Silently, I would answer if they thought of him great prior to the Khmer Rouge, they would think of him better in the way he conducted himself during the most dangerous time being a city kid during the Khmer Rouge. I could not talk about Baron without getting teary and choking up. In my eyes, he was the brother who saved my life. He taught me to be courageous. He taught me to be inventive when necessary to meet basic needs. The grasshoppers, the crickets, the snails, and any living things that he was able to catch were the extra protein he shared with me to keep the body functioning. Not only did he look out for me during tough times, but he also looked out for others. For this reason, he was the brother that I wished to be like.

My fourth and youngest brother was five years old when we evacuated from Phnom Penh. He loved dogs. Our family dog was his best friend. At five years old, Phirum did not need a babysitter. He just needed our dog. Our dog's name was Trop. It meant wealth or eggplant. The kinship between Phirum and Trop was strong. Phirum was kind and gentle. He was receptive to everything. He would not complain when he faced difficulty. He was the good kid that Mom and Dad adored.

Boys were common in our family. Besides having four brothers, I also had five uncles from Dad's side of the family and six uncles from Mom's side. My father was the oldest of seven, whereas my mother was the oldest of ten.

Even though he grew up in a male-dominated household, Dad did not display any aggressive behavior to consider himself strong. In fact, he was kind and gentle. He treated people the same way he treated us. Regarding discipline, my father refrained from using physical punishment, which is frequently employed by many parents. Perhaps he learned that this was the best way to discipline a child other than the old way that his parents and other parents used to hit or spank their children with a stick or a belt. Mom was the oldest of ten. She had her share of discipline from her father. She used to say that maternal grandfather Ros Sok used a belt to lash out his anger if she would not listen to him.

Whenever any one of us was naughty, Dad pretended not to notice. Mom would record our misbehavior in her eyes and demeanor to tell us how disappointed she was. We would not get away from it, of course. She had a thin stick made for the purpose of punishment. We would have to put out our hands to receive the spanking. Sometimes, Dad would raise his voice to scare us about disciplinary action, but he never did it.

Among us five children, I remember my brother Baron got the most spankings. It was not that he was mischievous. It was that he challenged the status quo. For example, if Mom asked him to do something, he would ask "why." He consistently asked for a clear explanation for each requirement. Or perhaps he was just against being told what to do by the adults with the authority. It had to make sense to him to do something, not just to comply without asking why, even though it came from the adults. Baron insisted on respect that was equal to all, irrespective of age, gender, or parental authority. There was no absolute obedience from him. Mom was not used to having a kid challenge her before. She used to be obedient herself. Therefore, she felt obliged to teach him how to be submissive. It failed because Baron considered parenting power unjust.

Mom was raised to obey and respect parents, people with positions of power, and elders in general. It was a blind respect without asking why. It was her generation. She felt compelled to follow the tradition.

Now that Mom had children of her own, discipline was part of her job. Dad never took the initiative to discipline us. He aimed to be the "good parent," while Mom was always the "bad cop." We were all more scared of Mom than of Dad. We retreated immediately when we got the stare from Mom. However, we giggled when Dad cleared out his vocal cords to show that he could be tough. Somehow, his face did not look mean, unlike Mom's. Dad used verbal threats with no action. Mom never said much. She tolerated more, but when she had enough, no one could get away from the punishment.

Mom learned from her father that without pain, one could not succeed. Being the oldest child, she had persevered. Her father took physical discipline literally. Mom was taught that the adults had all the answers. Obviously, children were not permitted to ask questions. The concepts of "do what I say and don't do what I do" was misguided and hypocritical in my view. I understood that Mom had been raised under strict discipline by her overbearing father but repeating the same approach with her own children did not align with the idea of progress. After all, she had received an education and had

11

the ability to approach things with reason. She excelled as a leader in her accounting career. Yet, she still abided by society that dictated the rules to be followed.

One thing I did not understand about punishment by spanking was the absolute power of the adult. When Baron got a spank, he cried. Baron cried because of not just the immediate pain but pride.

Mom was annoyed, and she whacked him some more for him to stop crying.

"Stop crying." She insisted.

"How can I stop if you keep on whacking me?" he spoke back. He got another one.

It did not make sense to me either. Why did Mom need him to stop crying for her to stop whacking? Did she need total submission? Baron had his pride, and so did Mom. More importantly, he challenged her authority. Mom believed that respect was to be obedience. We were taught to respect adults totally. We were never taught that respect was reciprocal or earned. At an early age, Baron wanted the right to earn respect. He determined to be unconventional. It was unfair that adults had all the rights and children had none. Was the teaching of Buddhism that gave rise to power of those in charge without check and balance? We were expected to respect elders without questioning them. There were no check and balance to the system of top down, allowing bad actors to use religion as righteousness without considering the consequence to their actions.

I watched Baron being punished quietly. Although I was not comfortable seeing the use of force to hurt children for disciplinary action, I chose to be a spectator. I already conformed to the norm, allowing parents to do what was best. I had no imagination of what a just society looked like. However, my brother, Baron, knew what he wanted. He questioned the status quo. He would not accept the norm that allowed parents to discipline children as it was done to them. He wanted to change the perception of how parents wanted the best for their children by allowing the children to know what they wanted for themselves.

Looking back, I was more impressed at my brother for his determination to change social norms starting from home. Mom used to say that Grandfather Sok would use his belt to discipline her and her brothers for sneaking out for a bike ride while they were to spend extra time after school reading. How was it that when Mom became the parent, she did what her father did to her? Didn't she feel compassion or pain toward her own children? Didn't she feel hurt when she got beat up? Mom was not a challenger. She believed that society was right to allow parents to shape their children for the better. She was an example of hard work and success.

Baron would not have it. While physical pain did not last long, his pride and dignity were in jeopardy. He would always want an explanation of how the act of violence would influence the result. In a nutshell, Baron gave Mom the most headaches out of us five children.

I was a conformer. I listened. I stayed away from trouble, unlike my brother, Baron. He was curious. He questioned the status quo. He wanted a reasonable explanation from the adults. He rejected the notion of "do as I say, not as I do." Whereas all I ever wanted was toys and nice dresses. Mom made dresses for me. Baron intended to enter the military and moved up in ranks. He had goals in military leadership. It was unheard of in our family to have a young boy unselfishly inspired for greatness.

On the other hand, father was not inspired by greatness. He wanted to be just a family man. He worked hard to support the family. During free time, he wanted to spend time with us. I recall the weekends spent enjoying a picnic in the countryside and watching a movie in the city. He loved entertaining family and friends. He loved to dance. There was not a dull moment having four boys and one girl in the house. All five of us were ten years old and under.

Mom came from a strict family. Her grandfather was educated and worked at the royal palace. They observed rules and had grand expectations for their children. Her father was stricter. It was all about doing things the right way according to their standard. She could never challenge the status quo. Having her own son question the difference between right and wrong in spanking was already a conflict. Mom was used to severe punishment even though she was not at all wrong. She was just replying without permission. Mom used to get more whacking on behalf of her younger siblings. She was expected to be good at school, caretaker of her younger siblings, clean, and cook. There were no questions asked.

I wondered if absolute power existed in the family and how much of the absolute power existed in the function of society. I was told that the authority given to the teacher was absolute.

"The teacher is always right." Mom confirmed.

"We cannot challenge their ideas." She spoke. Enormous power was given to the teacher. Why did the Khmer Rouge despise teachers if they themselves teachers? It did not make sense to me.

There was not a dull moment in our house. At the beginning of April, it was considered spring cleaning for Cambodia. I remember we cleaned the house until it shined to welcome the New Year angels and relatives.

Cambodia celebrates New Year with Lunar Calendar as well. However, the weather in Cambodia was difference. Farmers were not able to complete harvest on time for the celebration. Therefore, they put off New Year until Spring to enjoy time off longer after work was accomplished. April 13-16 became the dates to stop all production and unwind. This way they had more time with families and a bundle of goods to share.

Our home was crowded in April of 1975. I remember seeing my paternal grandparents, aunts, and uncles. They came to celebrate the New Year with us. Dad was the oldest son. He was kind and responsible. He enjoyed hosting events and seeing family members. There was nothing unusual that I could remember. It was the time of year when food was abundant. Afterward, we packed up and went to the countryside. It resembled an all-day picnic. Some adults went fishing and I remembered dad roasted the chicken. I was left to play with mud. It was like Play-Doh. It was like a red clay. I made tiny pots and pans with it. It was calm and felt so natural playing with dirt. It seemed like I was connected with mother earth.

No matter what the condition of the country at the time was, I never even once saw my dad lose his spirit. He enjoyed spending time with us, enjoyed the company of relatives and friends, and had a deep love for dancing. Whenever I asked those who knew him, they always shared fond memories of him. Dad had made such an impact on the people who knew him. Whenever my memories of my dad begin to fade away, I would ask people who knew him to describe to me what Dad was like. I would ask my aunts to tell me something they remembered about my father. What was he like? How did he treat you? What do you remember about him? Was he kind to you?

My aunt Dara was fifteen at the time. She had nothing but good memories of my dad.

"He was the best brother-in-law!" Aunt Dara exclaimed.

"In what way?" I asked.

"He devoted himself to his family. He was kind, dependable, and funny. Not to mention he was handsome." she continued.

It was the truth. I used to see how sharp he looked in a suit going to work in the morning. He was made for a white-collar job. There was a calm demeanor about him. His smile was gentle, and, more importantly, everyone could count on him.

"He was also generous. He would take us to see movies or eat out." Aunt Dara described how he would tease her over the man she was going to marry one day. He hoped she would marry a man as handsome as he was.

Aunt Dara would tell him that she would marry someone who would be "more handsome than you." Dad pretended that his ego got struck by Aunt's words. They would laugh hard together. Dad was at least two decades older than Aunt Dara. However, he could have a good relationship with just about any generation.

My father had a considerable impact on numerous individuals' lives. My mother was also the oldest child in her family. She had nine siblings. As the eldest daughter, she held the responsibility of caring for her younger siblings and was expected to serve as a role model for them. In addition to her increased duties, she was expected to do well in school. My mother also became the family seamstress. She repaired and modified various shirts, skirts, and pants for her younger siblings and assisted her mother with cooking regularly.

Mom used to tell me the story when she was fifteen and had to accompany her mother to the outdoor market. Grandma Mak Yay was skillful when it came to bargain hunting. She would take her time looking at the difference in freshness of day-old vegetables. She could get a cheaper price for days old, but she would have to cook right away.

She would do the same with fruits. Mak Yay had to. She cared for many children.

Mom would prefer that she buy less so that she does not need to carry a heavy basket. Back then, she had no refrigerator to store food. Therefore, early daily shopping became one of the chores that she had to help Mak Yay.

One day, while waiting for Mak Yay, Mom stood next to the freshwater seafood stall. As she watched Mak Yay bargaining and socializing with her regular vendor, she felt something cold and slimy climb over her feet.

"Ayy." She screamed. Her frightening voice carried to the entire block. Grandma came running to her side.

"What's wrong?" she asked frantically.

Mom pointed to the creature in the dirt. It was a freshwater eel about a foot long and three inches wide. It tried to escape the bucket that was not tall enough to keep the eel in.

Social Norm

Parents had ultimate rights to select potential suitors for their children. The teaching of respecting elders and authority figures gave absolute power to those who had bad intentions. It was "do as I say and not do as I do" parenting.

Fortunately, my parents were more sensible than most parents. Perhaps it was due to their educational backgrounds. They both went to the School of Commerce, a college established during the French colonization in Phnom Penh, Cambodia. Father began college earlier than Mother. He was in his senior year when mom began college. It was love at first sight for him. He pursued and waited for Mom to complete her degree.

It was still unacceptable for young people to choose their own spouse regardless of such an attraction. Parents were still the gatekeepers for each family. The best marriage was when both sides of the parents approved of the nuptial. It was still rare to allow adult children to make their own decisions when it came to marriage. Mom and Dad met their own challenge. Regardless of the difficulty, Mom and Dad defied the norm and chose each other.

Dad was a prodigy son. He never once made his parents worried about any misbehaving. Mom said that prior to marrying her, he used to give his entire salary to his mother for extra spending. His charm and social skills led many parents to propose marriage for their daughters. He even got the offer from his boss, a Chinese Cambodian tycoon.

Rumor had it that my paternal grandmother, Vanna, was thrilled with such proposals. She always knew that Dad's proper etiquette, humor, and charisma would allow him to climb the social ladder. She urged Dad to decide based on social status rather than happiness. However, Dad would never exchange his feelings for upward mobility. He was devoted to his mom. His security was his love, not money. He relied on his skills to support his family. Fortunately, he did not listen to his mom.

In contrast, my maternal grandparents did not object to the union. Perhaps, as the oldest daughter, Mom had proved worthy of the trust from her parents. Or perhaps she was educated enough that she knew what she wanted in a man, and her happiness was what they had hoped for.

Unlike Mak Yay, Vanna, paternal grandmother, did not approve of the marriage. She even refused to attend her favorite son's wedding. She believed happiness meant being wealthy. On the contrary, paternal grandfather Pol Juenn was thrilled to support the happiness of his eldest son. He was proud of his son for not being swayed by money or status. Moreover, the thought of maternal grandparents allowing Mom to choose a husband of her choice was liberating enough for him. Of course, Mom would never allow me to speak ill of my paternal grandmother. After five children and over a decade of being married to Dad, she forgave her mother-in-law. I mentioned the conflict with Grandmother Vanna because Baron and I were mistreated by her during the Khmer Rouge. I wanted to understand why she did what she did during the worse time of the country. We were her grandchildren. Yet, she failed to protect us. Apparently, she allowed her grudge to overshadow her kinship between us.

Although maternal grandparents allowed Mom to marry a man of her choice, my Aunt Fany did not get the same treatment. Even though she achieved remarkable results in school and became a professor of English, she was at the mercy of her parents when it came to marriage. She could not choose her high school sweetheart, yet she was promised to a noble family with great ancestry and land. He was twenty years older than her, with an exceptional background of generations serving in the military. He was the most patriotic individual I knew. While he served in the Cambodian Royal Navy as Commander, his only brother served as a fighter pilot in the Cambodian Royal Air Force.

Unlike Dad, Aunt Fany is a woman. She could not refuse her father. Mak Yay had little influence in the nuptial. Grandfather Ros made all the household decisions. Aunt Fany was the unhappy bride, but she complied with the social norm. In addition, she did not want to be "Kone Ott Poocj." It was her duty to listen to her parents.

While Grandmother Vanna did not recognize Mom as her daughter-in-law, Grandfather Pol adored and respected Mom. His son's happiness was all that mattered to him. Grandfather Pol was ready for a new era where women could achieve success in a working environment as well as men. He appreciated the fact that Mom and Dad could earn income, whereas Grandmother Vanna still believed that the woman's place was at home. Perhaps it was the real reason that she did not support her father's choice. It was not all about wealth. It was about the status quo.

Mom and Dad were brave enough to stand up against a society that dictated what was right and wrong according to the wishes of the parents. Children are considered "Kone Mean Pooch" if they listen and follow the directions of their parents. Fortunately, my parents were the generation that brought change to society. They stood up for their love only to be cut short by the Khmer Rouge.

Mom appreciated the fact that she got to go to school. It was the best opportunity for her future. Being the oldest of ten was not an easy childhood. However, she took every opportunity to better herself. It was because she saw how hard Mak Yay worked to support all the kids. The home they built together in Phnom Penh due to Mak Yay's ability to run a household with a limited budget to support all ten children. Mak Yay never complained because it was her dream to live in the city so that her children could attend school.

Mak Yay was born in 1920. Her parents were agriculturalists residing in a small town approximately sixty miles from Phnom Penh, near Kandal Province. Her mother died at a young age, leaving her father to manage by himself. She had three siblings. Her older brother had an accident and died at a youthful age without medical assistance. She only had the next oldest brother and a younger sister remaining. At the tender age of ten years, she took care of household responsibilities. She ensured regular meals for her father and younger sister after her brother was married.

As a woman, Mak Yay knew that she would be married one day. When she turned sixteen, suitors in town would come to ask her father for her hand in marriage. However, Mak Yay had a dream of her own. She wished to escape her provincial life in the countryside. If she could not be literate herself, she at least wished for her children to succeed in their own language. Mak Yay had always been a responsible young lady. Her wishes were possible should there be outside suitors in her own small town.

Fortunately, my great-grandfather Ros Enn loved the countryside. He enjoyed fishing, fresh air, and endless nature. He often left the city to visit his parent's hometown near Mak Yay's.

In hindsight, he was always looking out for an eligible bachelorette for his son, Ros Sok. When he came across Mak Yay, he had to make a deposit. He promised to build a house for the bride's family prior to the wedding. Mak Yay did not object to her father's arrangement with Ros Inn, for she knew her dream of living in the city so that she could learn what ways of life were in sight. Even though she did not get to meet the groom prior to the wedding, she had faith in the process.

Grandfather Ros Sok was the only son. He had certain privileges of being a man. There was great expectation of him to do what his father said and to uphold the tradition and value of being exposed to the teaching of the upper class and serving in the royal household. As he completed his education, he took the exam to join law enforcement. He served with customs and immigration agencies. Thus, he learned rules and etiquette, which he passed to his descendants.

Ros Sok went to law enforcement training and worked in the detective department under the French colonization. He had a sense of justice within him. He had responsibilities as a son, a husband, and a father. He ensured that they had a home in Phnom Penh where Mak Yay learned the city lifestyle and managed daily expenses on a budget given by his grandfather. They were married in the late 1930s.

Together, they had thirteen children, with ten reaching adulthoods.

Life in the city was not as simple as the countryside. As a young bride, she had to learn proper etiquette, rules, and food that was available only for the upper class. Mak Yay needed to acquire extensive knowledge in order to impart it to her daughters. It was the reason Mom was versatile when it came to her skills. In addition to her white-collar profession, she possessed the skills of a seamstress and cook, capable of creating various types of clothing.

Becoming a young adult in America, I learned to focus on what I could do best. It required more effort to use my energy to learn many things, which reduced the likelihood of mastering any one thing. As a young refugee, mastering the English language and accessing job opportunities was my priority. Yet, Mom attempted to impose her belief in being a graceful young lady on me.

For example, at home, on some occasions, I skipped around the house. I dragged my feet when walking. One could hear the sound from the clothes I wear when I walk quickly. Of course, I did not hear it because I did not pay attention to it. Mom would come out with her stare and comment.

"A proper young lady does not make a sound as she walks. She would be called Kon-Jer-Tloose." Kon-Jer-Tloose translates directly to "the hole in a basket." Figuratively, it meant a lady was without dignity. A hole represented the emptiness of the core value inside. It was like a basket referred to the lady. It implied that a young woman would not be trustworthy or proficient enough to manage a household if she had flaws.

In my early twenties, I often argued with Mom. I did not understand the rules she was trying to impose on me. I clearly made it known to her that I exist in a different environment than when she was growing up. Maybe she worried I couldn't handle such freedom alone. Or perhaps she was afraid of what was out there. I took her cautionary comments as a restriction to my newfound liberation. I was determined to work hard to achieve my independence so that I would not be molded by Mom's perception of how a young woman should behave.

I acknowledged undergoing internal and external changes. I was in short supply of patience. I viewed Mom's effort of wanting me to be graceful as irritation. At the time, I expected so much of myself. When I saw fellow high school graduates moving on to university away from home, I wanted to be like them. I was craving independence. At the same time, I had yet to master the English language to achieve the grade level that allowed me the chance to explore. I settled for community college because it was all my mom could afford. Besides, it was a better option for me to learn anyway. I thrived, and I achieved in every class I attended, except chemistry. The subject was not my cup of tea.

Formidable Decision

When the going gets tough, flee. For the person on the top, like Prime Minister Lon Nol, the decision to leave Cambodia as news of the Khmer Rouge victory was near was the only solution. Certainly, he and his family had already been granted asylum to enter the United States. He did make a great deal with the United States as he closed his eyes to the U.S. bombing during the Vietnam War. It was the U.S. and North Vietnam that used Cambodia very well to their advantage. Unfortunately, no one considered the consequence of the results either way. For the U.S., it was less consequence. While Vietnam achieved its goal, Cambodia was thrown into an unknown political circumstance where no one from the outside cared to give a damn. When it comes to civil war, no one from the outside world wanted to interfere. How bad could it be? The situation is dire. After all, it was their fellow Cambodians. No one expected that the Khmer Rouge intended to rid the country of those who were influenced by the outside world and had knowledge.

Weeks prior to April 17, 1975, Phnom Penh was chaotic. The roads closure was in every direction outside of the city. Traveling by automobile was no longer possible. Air travel was grounded severely. However, few domestic flights remained active to other provinces. Suddenly, wealth could no longer be the tool to safety. Air transportation was only available to those who could be trustworthy.

Mom's sister, Fany, and her family were trapped in Phnom Penh after attending the funeral of her father-in-law. She and her family had to go back home to Riem province. There was no way out by land from Phnom Penh. She scouted everywhere for domestic plane tickets. Dad secured several seats on a flight to Riem. My brother, Virak, Mak Yay, and other young uncles were included. Dad said that we were going to meet them later. He could not leave with his parents and brothers, who were still staying with us over the Cambodian New Year.

Aunt Fany was grateful for Dad's assistance in securing her alternate flight. Dad used his personal connection to ensure that she got to leave the city of Phnom Penh. It was a time when money could not buy accessibility to quick transportation. It was a relationship and trustworthy individual who could secure an escape route. Dad had an option to live with the rest of our families. However, being the responsible adult, he had to consider his elder parents and other siblings who had no idea or the direction of what this civil war would ensure their safety. Fortunately, he allowed my older brother, Varik, to leave first, including Mak Yay and Mom's younger siblings.

"Without his help, we could not get back to Riem." I listened intensely. At the same time, I was thrilled to know how resourceful my father was at that time.

"I don't know how he did it." Aunt Fany was still in awe of his ability to connect with people. She had all the money, but she could not buy transportation back home.

Additionally, Aunt Fany shared with me the horrific experience of how she barely escaped from Phnom Penh. Her flight took off the ground successfully. As it was climbing, Aunt Fany happened to look back down. What she saw was devastating. An explosion hit the runway. Fortunately, the altitude of the plane reached the safety zone where no blast from the ground could bring the plane down. Pochentong International Airport in Phnom Penh, as she knew it, was now destroyed. She was shocked and anxious as she watched her family, and many others avoid danger. She only hoped that no one else looked down to bear witness to the brutality and the uncertainty of the country. For those airplanes that did not get to take off, she could only hope that the people were spare.

Aunt Fany lived in Riem, her home near the Naval base on a coastline to the Pacific Ocean in Cambodia. Once they landed, she and her husband had to make the ultimate decision. To leave or to stay was the question at hand, especially after they witnessed such a catastrophe during take-off at Phnom Penh airport.

Her husband had a strong patriotic heritage. He served in the Navy, climbing the chart of high-ranking officers, where his brother served in the Air Force as a fighter pilot. Deciding to flee the country was not on his agenda. However, Aunt Fany was adamant about what was at stake. She insisted that they had to leave to ensure the future of their daughters and those under their care.

Aunt Fany added that his decision to leave came with a standoff with other military personnel. It was about taking the ship for the escape. Finally, they worked out a compromise about who stayed and who was leaving. Altogether, three ships set out to sea with thousands of family members on board for each soldier and officer. The act of treason was there. However, the absence of top leaders seemed justifiable. It was a matter of survival.

Mak Yay was among the group with my older brother, three younger sons, and the comfort of having Aunt Fany, her husband, Khiev Kimtel, and her own son, Komsan and his family who were educated with other officers in the Navy. Their journey was now one of seeking refuge. Leaving their country was not an easy choice, but it was a necessary step to regroup until they had the intelligence to return safely to their post. For months, they survived at sea alongside thousands of others, including elders and children, in three ships.

Aunt Fany recalled that they requested refuge in Thailand. To their surprise, Thailand turned them down after taking valuable resources from top commandant. They had no choice but to continue at sea without a proper destination. They hoped to be rescued and for someone to understand the situation that they were in, homeless, country less. They reached international water where the U.S. told them to surrender their military ships. The U.S. escorted them to a Philippine port, where they were processed as refugees. Eventually, they were cleared to enter the U.S. via Camp Pendleton in 1975. Starting over without any news from families in Cambodia was agonizing.

However, life had to move on. All individuals had to adjust to the new environment and diligently work to support their families, regardless of their previous roles. Fortunately, Aunt Fany was already proficient in English that she was able to find work to support the family.

Nevertheless, she honored my father's generosity and kindness by remembering how efficient he was in obtaining plane tickets for them to escape Phnom Penh. As a result, Dad also saved his own son, Virak, who came to America at ten years old.

Chapter Two
The Khmer Rouge Regime

The twentieth century was a traumatic century for humanity to endure. Only humans could disrupt the normalcy of each society. Millions of individuals were left feeling exhausted, disoriented, homeless, drained, fearful, skeptical, and weary. The traumatic events included Armenia, the Holocaust, the Cambodian genocide under the Khmer Rouge, Kurds-Iraq, Rwanda, Bosnia/Kosovo, and Darfur.

I was just a kid when I became one of the victims of such an event. The ordeal left such a big hole in my heart. How can I ever forget the ugly side of humanity?

The thought of April 17, 1975, left me numb and speechless. I could never imagine I could live to tell my story of how I endured the great destruction of humanity for almost four years. How could I not hold such despair and resentment toward the adults who could have prevented such brutality from happening in Cambodia? It took eight long years for my mom and me to finally find refuge in America, eight years of waiting to reunite with our family. At the same time, those years felt like they had aged both my body and soul. To truly come to terms with my trauma, I had to look back, piece together the fragments of my past, and understand how they shaped the person I am today.

Historical Background

From its inception in the year 802, the Indigenous Khmer people were proven to be great. It was under King Jayavarman II that the Khmer Empire began to form one of its captivating historical movements. Under his leadership, the Khmer Empire made great strides in architectural innovation. It was the best construction ever for the city and religious observation. It was during this period of glory that the Khmer people saw peace and prosperity. It was called the Angkor Period between the ninth century to the thirteenth century (Vecchia, 2007). Each King Jayavarman expanded on the innovation of the past King. King Jayavarman VII built Angkor Thom.

Procrastination and complacency led to the decline. Between the 13th to 15th centuries, invasions by the newly grown neighboring countries were inevitable. There was no honor among thieves. Angkor Wat fell multiple times (Vecchia, 2007).

There was no break trying to defend the nation. The crisis persisted from the 16th to 19th centuries. Between those centuries, the Khmer people endured the control of Thailand, Vietnam, Emperor of Japan, and the French. However, the French presented themselves as the "protectorate" and colonizer eventually. To negotiate a ceasefire and end the aggression between both sides, the French proposed expanding the borders of Thailand and Vietnam, granting each country a portion of Khmer territory. The goal was to prevent further invasions. It was remarkable how the French had the power to give away land that was never theirs to begin with. It did not explain the decision to the Khmer people to achieve peace. Instead, it proposed a name change from the Khmer Empire to Cambodia, erasing the history of mass land in the Southeast Asia region.

More importantly, no one took advantage of Cambodia than the French. To ensure an ongoing relationship and influence, the French chose to install the nineteenth-year-old descendant of the monarchy, Norodom Sihanouk, out of the most qualified royal descendant. As colonizers and a disguised protector of the land, the French took more than they gave in return. Nothing was free. To acquire revenue, the French tapped into resources from the land, such as the best soil to grow the best rice in the world, rubber, provinces with priceless stones, and so forth. To quickly collect such revenues, they brought in Chinese business investors to Cambodia. They also brought Vietnamese civil servants to run their colonized administration. It would take longer to train the Khmer people to lead in the economy and government because most Khmer people were not educated. They were never taught to compete in business or to want more. The French only wanted to increase the nation's GDP because it would mean high revenue for them to take home. Therefore, the French had to import skilled individuals to run the country (Kiernan, 2004).

The Khmer Rouge

I am forever haunted by the words "Khmer Rouge." When I heard anyone mention the words, tears immediately filled my eyes. I tried to understand the significance of the words that made me feel sad. The word "Khmer" refers to the nationality and language. Khmer is the original identity of the Indigenous Khmer people. Rouge is a French word meaning red. Again, why red? My thought of the name Khmer Rouge was more sinister than the people and the color red. Was the intention of the Khmer Rouge to spill blood? Did it anticipate murdering certain groups of people? Sihanouk reportedly coined the term "Khmer Rouge" to describe the Khmer communists (Becker, 1986). Or was the "Rouge" inspired by the Chinese cultural revolution? The Khmer Rouge's policy was inspired by Maoism. I wondered why this Chinese communism came to flourish after Sihanouk spent decades crushing communist ideology and attacking any political rivals from existence.

Many of the Khmer Rouge leaders originated from a group of educators. They leveraged the resources at their disposal to undertake their academic pursuits in France. In addition to their academic career, they also joined the membership with the French Communist party (Chandler, 1999). After returning home, they became involved with the

Indochina Communist Party (ICP). The desire to improve society and the country appeared to rest with those who viewed communism and socialism as the only means of preserving authenticity and resisting foreign exploitation. They harbored deep resentment toward foreigners and the geopolitical interference in their nation. They dreamed of returning Cambodia to its roots, where the population consisted mainly of Indigenous Khmer who farmed and lived off the land, without literacy in their language, which existed for thousands of years. How was it possible? The population had changed. There were several instances of incursions from Thailand and Vietnam, with some individuals choosing to remain settled as a result of marriages. A significant number of Chinese immigrants were brought in by the French to bolster economic growth. They were the largest group occupied in Cambodia during the French colonization. Therefore, the population of Cambodia at the time was diverse including the Cham (Muslim) people.

The Khmer Rouge began to adopt Mao Zedong's Cultural Revolution and the communist ideology of transforming Cambodia into an agrarian utopia (Short, 2004). It was extremist thinking. They began by disassociating themselves from Western influence and ideology. They wanted to "reeducate" the population. In other words, they wanted to cultivate a population to get rid of personal values, including knowing who they were as individuals. It was like reengineering a machine, not a human.

The Khmer Rouge Leadership

Who would have thought that the evils among us were those we trust and respect? The teachers. I was brought up to believe that teachers were equal to parents. We had to give the same respect and obedience just like our parents. Teachers were អ្នកមានគុណ.

Teachers were នាក់មានគុណ (Nak Meen Konh) just like parents. They were people that we children were supposed to be grateful for. Yet, they became the biggest betrayers of them all. Instead of teaching us values, integrity, and hard work, they taught us to hate. While the elite pursued greater wealth and politicians clung to power, the working class was consumed with the struggle to support their families. Meanwhile, bad actors exploited the nation's vulnerabilities, its spirit, mind, and heart. No one seemed to care about the country's future; they were all too absorbed in their own self-righteous pursuits. The Khmer Rouge leaders executed their plan when they observed weaknesses within the current administration. Once belonging to the educational elite, Saloth Sar, Khieu Thirith, and Khieu Ponnary put their plan into action.

They saw the polluted culture that they wanted to change, yet they knew no bounds when it came to possession of power. I was in awe when I learned that among the Khmer Rouge leadership were women. I wondered what kind of parents they would make. At the same time, I was shocked to find that they were also educators at one point. They were the bad actors that brought Cambodia down to its knees.

Khieu Thirith and Khieu Ponnary were the daughters of a Judge in Cambodia. Kaing Khek Iev (Deuch) was a schoolteacher. Khieu Samphan was once a member of parliament and minister under Sihanouk in 1962. He earned a PhD in economics. Ieng Sary was a member of the French Communist Party. He married Khieu Thirith. His real name was Kim Trang. Other deputy Khmer Rouge regimental commanders, Hun Sen and Heng Samrin, fled to Vietnam in 1977 and in 1978 (Short, 2004).

Saloth Sar. I was furious when I learned that the infamous name Pol Pot, known as "Brother Number One," the supreme leader, the mastermind behind the Khmer Rouge, was not his real name. He was born as Saloth Sar. How dare he choose the last name, Pol. I hated the man with all my might. Did the name Pol sound authentically Khmer? What and who did he try to convince when he chose the alias "Pol." My assumption is that he aimed to appeal to the Indigenous and rural population native to Cambodia, excluding influences from the Chinese and Vietnamese ethnic composition that impacted urban society. Or perhaps he randomly selected a name that was not his own to commit such a horrendous crime against humanity. Did he assume that no one would find out who he really was? What drove a man to believe that what he did was for the greater good of the country? Was his life that terrible for him to want to change society in that ill manner? Did he not consider that I have to live knowing what he did to my family?

According to my reading, his life was not at all terrible. He seemed to live better than the average Cambodian. His family-owned farmland. His cousin was connected to the royal court. He got access to the noble families and court. He got the opportunity to study in France. He was one of the educators in the country. Yet, he acted like he had been deprived of love and neglected by society, which led him to choose the direction where he could gain power and make those who wronged him pay for his suffering. It did not make sense to me that if a guy wished to have power and acknowledgment, why didn't he use his own birth name?

He changed his name to hide his true identity, following the example of communist leaders like Lenin, Stalin, Tito, and Ho Chi Minh (Chandler, 1999). It was the way to stay off the radar of the secret intelligent bad actors list.

It was interesting to me when author Chandler (1999) stated that communist leaders took pseudonyms to inspire their followers like Stalin meant "Steel" and Ho Chi Mind meant "the enlightened one." Who did Saloth Sar want to inspire? Rural folks? Uneducated folks? The Khmer

Rouge's goal was to make Cambodia "pure" again. It was his belief that multi-ethnic groups corrupted the country and the people. He likely chose the name Pol Pot because it was familiar to the Khmer people. Apparently, he wanted to be authentic to the original Khmer ancestry. He wanted the rural Khmer to know that he was one of them. I have heard from the elders that my paternal great-grandfather and grandfather were leaders in their hometown in the countryside with unwavering characters and humble nature. Perhaps, Saloth Sar wanted to earn such a reputation to choose the name of my ancestor.

This was feasible. I often wondered how my grandfather, father, and three uncles would feel if they knew that a madman was using their family name and was responsible for their demise. I also wondered what Saloth Sar's tombstones transcribed. Was it Pol Pot or Saloth Sar? How did he want to be remembered? The fact that he was known by the world as a notorious person who led the Khmer Rouge to exterminate millions of people. In my mind, the name was not real. Did he choose Pol Pot to protect his family or himself? Most likely, he wanted to protect himself. In that case, he was a coward in my view. I wondered what his family thought of him. Was he a hero in their eyes? I read somewhere that he did have children. What did he pass on to them? Many adult survivors expressed hatred for the Khmer Rouge but did not mention hating Pol Pot.

It appeared that I was the only one who despised Saloth Sar for using the name Pol Pot. It was because he tarnished the good name of my ancestors. I also hated the fact that people looked at me strangely when they heard the last name "Pol." For sure, in their minds, they were skeptical if I was related to Pol Pot or not. The name "Pol" also triggered trauma for many survivors. It was unfortunate that no one paused to understand that the name Pol Pot was a pseudonym. Mom made sure that I knew Pol Pot was not a real name.

In High School, my name caused me some trauma. World history class was about WWI and WWII. Yet, the teacher appeared knowledgeable about global issues beyond WWI and WWII history. On that first day of class, it was a roll call.

"Socheata Pol?" a Caucasian world history teacher called out my name with curiosity. Perhaps he knew about the Khmer Rouge, but it was not enough. I raised my hand up high in leu to answer "Yes." I raised my hand instead of answering. I was also shy and nervous at the beginning of every class.

"Are you in any relation to Pol Pot?" he asked bluntly. It was then that I felt uncomfortable. I wanted to say "no," but nothing came out of my lip. The lump I felt in my throat was so big that I felt choking. I was traumatized. I fought back tears from bursting out. It would be embarrassing if I cried uncontrollably. Most students would not know or understand my background anyway. I needed to persevere in order to successfully complete the course. I did not think that they cared about who Pol Pot was. I stood still, numbed, not able to utter out the word "No."

Noticing the uncomfortable moment, the teacher proceeded to the next student in roll call. It was in 1987. Since then, I have begun to be aware of my last name. When people ask for my name, I would only say my first name. When I met Cambodian families or people, I was more cautious about telling them my full name until they asked specifically. It was my trauma, and I did not know it.

The Perfect Storm

Following the conclusion of the Vietnam War, the Khmer Republic under Lon Nol experienced a decline in strength, which facilitated the progression of the Khmer Rouge. There was no more support from the U.S. At the same time, there was no interference from foreigners like there was nothing happen in the region years ago. The casualties of war nearby were forgotten. The decision makers prioritized their beliefs over the consequences of their actions. Many embassies began to evacuate including the U.S. embassy leaving on April 12, 1975.

The Khmer Rouge's victory came as a surprise to city folks. It was almost unexpected that the revolution, which was operating in the jungle, found its way into all the cities effortlessly. It was like the stars aligned in perfect unison. The opportunity was there to be taken. Perhaps, people were tired of fighting. They lacked knowledge regarding the Khmer Rouge and their objectives. Yet, they accepted the new government without question. There was no more resistance. It is plausible that the population had grown discontented with the former leadership to such an extent that the identity of the new leader was secondary; the primary concern was the necessity for a change in leadership.

It was common knowledge that the existing government under Prime Minister Lon Nol was weak, corrupted, and influenced by foreigners. Therefore, the Khmer Rouge appealed to the average people who thought that their miseries were due to the exploitation and overbearing of external forces. Somehow, people were desperate for new leadership and new political parties, and they failed to understand the purpose. They blindly assumed that what was to come would be better than the existing injustice. After all, they were sick of the class system and the huge gap in equity and justice. I was overwhelmed when I learned that both of my grandfathers had retired from decades of careers in law enforcement. Mom's great-aunt was the first woman chief surgeon in medical school; my uncles were ranking officers in the Cambodian Navy; my aunt was an English professor; both of my parents held leadership positions within manufacturing companies; and my mom's younger adult siblings were in college. Yet, no one in my family had knowledge of the Khmer Rouge and their intention. Many Cambodian adults of that generation accepted the new government to end the war without question. Or maybe they believed it was a shift in governing ideology that remained acceptable, as it served the country's and people's best interests.

I once asked Mom, "Have you ever voted?" Mom thought for a moment, then said. "No."

Mom and Dad believed in the good of others. They did not expect that their own fellow citizens would be deceitful and evil. They complied with the request to vacate their residence for reorganization without raising any inquiries. They only prepared enough supplies to last days. They did not expect the lie from the beginning, although the violent response to those who refused to leave their homes was obvious. It was not a choice. It was an order. Therefore, we all marched out of our homes without destination. Mom and Dad did their best to ensure our safety during the exodus.

After all, the loudspeaker ordered residents to leave without worrying about heavy packing. The recommendation for packing was for three days only while the city would undergo reconstruction for a new government.

Mom and Dad believed the message completely. Dad thought of politics as usual. He did not anticipate the violence and cruelty being deployed on one another. He did not expect that it was also a judgment day for those who refused to leave their homes.

Perhaps, Dad misunderstood the objective of the Khmer Rouge as well. He was puzzled about making the country equal through strict policy. He did not know of the primary motive behind the Khmer Rouge. It was obsession. It was about retaining one ethnic group, the Khmer.

How else would they begin by eliminating ethnic minorities from the entire country? At the same time, they began to remove educators, professionals, artists, religious leaders, and even students from their positions. They did it to convince the average people of reorganization to allow equality and to have no class system in the society as they promised.

Supposedly, the purpose of the revolution was to restore justice to those who had been neglected by society for so long. Yet, the act of suppressing knowledgeable individuals and opposing viewpoints to control independent thinkers was the act of a frailty individual.

Ironically, the Khmer Rouge leaders were among the educators, including several members of the elite class. The Khmer Rouge leaders used the opportunity to do evil for their own benefit. While the average people in society were too busy going about their daily lives because they were taught to respect class system and titles without using their common sense to understand the purpose and to perceive the impact of what might have been if they neglected moral ethics.

A communist's ideology always preached equality. They promised to level the playing field so that there would be no top and bottom. They promised to create a society of equality was just a fallacy. If equality was the aim why began by separating city folks and rural folks. Why were rural folks having more authority and privileges than the city folks? Why was it necessary to identify status and roles in the previous administration before starting a new society of equality? I found their propaganda to be faulty. How was that equal? It was interesting how they abandoned the usage of words relating to titles and ranks by the order of ages. The

Khmer Rouge had me learned to call everyone, "Mett." The word means "friend." It would reflect equality according to the revolution.

It was intriguing to observe the Khmer Rouge's attempt to implement the Year Zero concept, similarly to the French Revolution. Year Zero for the French Revolution marks the overthrow of the French Monarchy on September 20, 1792. The French executed the entire monarchy's descendants to begin a new revolution. Unlike the French, the Khmer Rouge did not execute Prince Sihanouk because, after all, he contributed to the success of the revolution. It was the innocent people that paid the hefty price including children and elderly adults.

If the concept behind Year Zero was to eliminate the existing cultures and traditions in order to build new ones, why kill? A new society can be built without the destruction of human lives. However, the Khmer Rouge sought absolute power, driven by deep-seated hatred and envy toward those who had once controlled the nation. The marginalized felt excluded from the very society and country to which they belonged. In their disillusionment, they found empowerment in a new system where they had previously held no stake. The root of evil began when ignorance was put in charge. Did the Khmer Rouge leaders do that intentionally? After all, they were a group of educators who had the privilege to study in France. If they were educated in the right way, they would at least understand that Plato and Socrates agreed that ignorance was the stem of all evil.

Evacuation

The chaos and confusion surrounding the infamous day of April 17, 1975, was due to the harshness of the revolution. The Khmer Rouge deployed young soldiers with no compassion and understanding to rid people in the cities. Phnom Penh was the target site. Mom and Dad accepted the new government. They, too, wanted a classless society where equality for all was possible. However, it was puzzling when the new government demanded that people leave their homes temporarily to restructure the city and government. The most alarming evidence was terminating at will for those who refused to leave their home as ordered.

Mom and Dad had no choice but to pack us up as quickly as they could. Dad's family was staying with us for the Cambodian New Year beginning on April 13. At the time, Dad was able to put us four kids in the jeep with his father and mother. The rest of the adults walked behind the jeep. There was no space for the car to be driven. Dad used it to ensure that we would not get lost in the crowd. In the myth of confusion, fear, and uncertainty, my youngest brother forgot to make sure that our dog was by his side.

As we proceeded down the road away from our home, my brother, Phirum, called out to our dog. We all saw her racing towards us. To our astonishment, the Khmer Rouge soldier shot our beloved dog. We were devastated. Phirum was beside himself with grief. Our family dog and he had a history together. We were never the same at that moment. The journey away from Phnom Penh was filled with challenges. I still had a vision of how Dad felt off the ship during the transport to our new location. We were forced into a cargo ship just like livestock. Somehow, Dad was pushed off the ramp. I did not see how he got back up, but to be reunited with him after we reached our destination was relief enough.

We were settled somewhere remote in Pursat Province. We were surrounded by the forest. It was an inhabitant environment before campgrounds were made for us.

Mom worried about her four younger siblings. They stayed in the city alone because of school. They did not go to Riem province with Mak Yay. Her younger sister, Dara, was fifteen years old. Her brother Veasna was seventeen. Her other brother, Serey, was nineteen. Finally, her other sister, Chanty, was twenty-two. She was in her second year of medical school. They were young and single. Being the oldest, Mom could not help but wish they had evacuated to the place they knew.

New People

If the Khmer Rouge intended to equalize the playing fields by abolishing the class system, why begin by dividing us into groups?

My family and I were referred to as newcomers because we came from Phnom Penh. Maybe we were assessed to determine if we fit the targeted classes. Prior to the revolution, Cambodian society was stratified into two classes: the lower class, comprising individuals who were poor and lacked formal education. The upper class consisted of officials and royal families. There was no middle class.

Being branded as new people, we were second-class citizens. We had no rights. We were stripped of any possessions, including family. I remember being bullied because I did not know the difference between fish. At the children's camp, I was also taught the Khmer Rouge's famous phrase.

ទុកមិនចំណេញ ពុកចេញមិនខាត

"To keep you is No gain; To lose you is No loss."

It was the slogan that we had to memorize. It was a threat. It reminded us to remain obedient. It reminded us of every day that our lives were expendable. I remembered.

Old People

Everyone from rural areas was labeled as "old people." The term "old" referred to the native population that lived free from politics, capitalism, and greed. They were people just like my grandmother. Many did not consider education to be necessary for living a peaceful life. They were already at peace until the tragedy of wars began. With their limited grasp of the arts of persuasion, they thought the revolution would restore justice and eliminate corruption in the country. They were willing to assist the Khmer Rouge in removing foreign influence. They also had no choice but to be willing participants.

The "Old People" had privileges and access to food in most areas. They were primarily the Khmer Rouge community leaders. I am still traumatized by the black uniforms and red "krama" (scarves). They had to accuse people of going against Angka's rules without evidence, and people got killed. It was hatred and bias toward the people who used to have more than those who now became the revolution leaders. They disdained city dwellers. It was like a game to watch the people who used to have everything and begged and worked to just earn the minimum rice ration to survive daily. There was no freedom for the new people to move around the camp, but the old people could because they had privileges.

It had been good for the old people. I wondered what happened to many of them who chose to participate in committing crimes against children by disregarding their common sense and Buddha's teaching since birth about doing no harm and respecting the lives of all living things. I wondered about the opportunists who gathered wealth by trading a cup of rice or sometimes a spoon of rice for a teaspoon of salt, sugar, or any food for any type of jewelry, such as diamonds and gold, in the underground market. These were items that the new people were able to hide. I wondered which Khmer Rouge leaders had all the wealth that they took away from innocent people after they left their homes. It was better to be the old people during the Khmer Rouge.

Ignorance Is Bliss

After the Khmer Rouge regime, I often heard people say, "Ignorance is bliss." I wondered if it was true or if it was an excuse.

I noticed that the people who said ignorance was blessed had their families in tack, while those deemed knowledgeable got their families destroyed.

I used to envy those families that did not lose anyone during the Khmer Rouge. They were mostly parents without or limited education in Cambodia. I wondered whether I would have suffered the loss of a father and three brothers if my parents had no education and were blue-collar workers. Would I appreciate the words ignorance was blessed?

It was because I saw how the Khmer Rouge protected the rural groups without education and persecuted those who spent their time learning so they could contribute to the country's economy.

I was confused by the backward thinking. As I searched for answers, I realized that the strategy of keeping people ignorant was for the benefit of the tyrants or oppressors. How else could they control people? The Khmer Rouge leaders took advantage of such individuals. They used fear and assigned blame to get people with limited understanding of how the world worked to get rid of one another. They told lies about all educators being corrupted. They blamed people who were born in the city, including children like me. I was being hated without knowing what I did wrong.

My own people persecuted me for no good reason. When I watched my brothers die one by one, I was beyond sadness.

I was infuriated. How could any adult allow such a thing to happen to children?

How could anyone believe that children like me deserved to die from starvation and overwork? I could have survived if I had been allowed freedom to look for food. It was intentional death by depriving children of access to nutrients. Yet, the Khmer Rouge expected children to work. The contradictory concept during the Khmer Rouge left me more confused than ever.

What remains true to me is the fact that the Khmer Rouge used uneducated people to conduct their executions. We encountered severe repercussions due to our urban backgrounds.

There was no question asked. What happened to the rights and wrongs that they were taught from generations of Buddhism to do no harm to others? How could one believe that saving a nation requires sacrificing another group?

There was no shame for the Khmer Rouge leaders to use ignorant people for their own political agenda. They exploited innocent minds because they were easier to convince. Informed and moral individuals would question these decisions. Thus, it was ideal for the population feeling abandoned and having little to lose. For this reason, I noted that society often overlooks the significance of individuals regardless of their backgrounds. Access to education for all would allow people to feel valued and that they could matter as a contributing factor to society. Instead, the society that I learned prior to the Khmer Rouge was not conducive to growth, which allowed such a twisted revolution to flourish.

I could not accept the term "ignorance is bliss." I have noticed survivors who were not educated during the Khmer Rouge use this phrase often to justify why their families stayed intact. It was due to their unfortunate circumstance of not being able to have an education and to live in rural areas other than the cities. I wondered why that would even matter. Did they not even have a conscience when other was killed and abused because they came from the city and were exposed to civility? Or did they say the phrase to justify their guilt and shame for not stepping up to help others when they knew the conduct of the Khmer Rouge was immoral and evil?

Ignorance was far from bliss, if it were, Mak Yay would never have longed for an education. Born a girl in a small town, she had no access to learning. In the early twentieth century, society was still unkind to women, leaving a girl from a rural village with no opportunity to read, write, or experience the power of words. Mak Yay was determined to change the outcome of her life. As she came of age, she was the caretaker of her family. Her mother died at an early age, leaving her to ensure the well-being of her father, a farmer, and other siblings. She cooked and cleaned. She nurtured everyone. Yet, she was not allowed to pursue her own dream of being literate. When it came the time when suitors came knocking on every young woman's household Mak Yay stated her demands on her father.

"He must be educated." She made herself clear to future suitors. She did not want to remain in a small town where she could not learn new things. She wanted to enrich her life by being in the city. She was a dreamer. She had a vision. She sought more from her life than being a farmer's wife, a common role for many small-town women.

When the offer of marriage came from a prominent, educated family, she had no choice but to accept it.

Her young life was transformed as she moved to the city and built a family at the turn of the twentieth century. Between the ages of nineteen and forty, Mak Yay delivered thirteen babies. When Mom had my older brother and me within a year of each other, Mak Yay was still having my uncles within a year of each other as well.

Although Mak Yay delivered thirteen babies, only ten survived. Mom is the oldest. She worked hard every day to ensure that her children received the education that she never did. As the eldest of ten, Mom was experienced in helping her mother with siblings, chores, and homework after school. Mom said that the educational system in Cambodia back then was all memorization. Multiple tables had to be recited in front of the class. Words, grammar, and concepts were evaluated often. Analytical thinking was limited.

Mom was so good with numbers that she became an accountant. She was hired right after college. There, she worked her way up to a leadership position within her department. The brother after her, Komsan, was equally successful in school. He chose to enter military school. He became an officer in the Marines. He even got a chance to study in the United States via military training collaboration. My Aunt Fany was noted to be the smartest one as well. She was fluent in English by the time she finished college. She loved Khmer literature and languages. Once college was done, she became the only English professor on her campus. My aunt, Chanty, was in medical school in 1975. Her education got cut short. Uncles Serei and Veasna were in college and in their late teenage years. Aunt Dara was turning eighteen. Luckily, Uncle Komsan and Fany's families, Mak Yay, three younger uncles, and my oldest brother escaped the Khmer Rouge in time. Unfortunately, Mom's family, Aunt Chanty and Dara, Uncle Serei and Veasna, and maternal grandfather were trapped in the Khmer Rouge.

Again, my thought went back to why ignorance is bliss. The Khmer Rouge's leadership was made up of educators, and yet they persecuted educated people. It did not make sense to me.

While ignorance might have been blessed, ignorance led to great atrocities because no one dared to question the morality of the order.

Before he died in 1998, Pol Pot told the media, "Everything I did, I did for my country." I was angry at his last words that were recorded. How dare he use the country to justify his evil mind? How dare he sacrifice millions of people for the need to feel better about himself? It was his retribution. For years, he had felt inferior, and now he sought to eliminate those he blamed for his suffering. He believed that to build something new, the old had to be sacrificed. Targeting those who had served under the French, he condemned Lon Nol's administration as traitors. He harbored deep resentment toward opportunists, Chinese and Vietnamese immigrants who, in his eyes, had gained wealth through skill and greed. He was a paranoid man. He could not distinguish between right and wrong if he believed in Buddha what was his judgment. What was his karma? It was reported that he died quietly because of his poor health. I was disappointed. If he were to say "sorry" for what he did, my heart would feel less pain, and my spirit would see a bright light. It would be easier for me to forgive. Unfortunately, Saloth Sar broke down the foundation of the Khmer people. We used to trust each other completely. We used to care for one another. Kindness and compassion no longer existed after the Khmer Rouge. Yet, we drew to the same language and culture, but with any sign of difference of opinion, we became estranged from one another. We could no longer trust the individual, including our own family. This was the legacy of the Khmer Rouge. It was the deception and the manipulation of the revolution that left people fearful of each other.

There are hundreds of books about vicious accounts of what happened during the Khmer Rouge regime between 1975 to 1979. The most famous one is about Dith Pran, whose story came to life in the movie *The Killing Fields*. I could not watch the movie in its entirety. I watched the ending. I loved the song "Imagine" by John Lennon. It was powerful and hopeful.

In addition, Mom converted her notes from the refugee camp into a book with the help of her writing classmate. She was afraid that her memories of such an unforgivable event would disappear if she did not act quickly. Her book is called *Vantha's Whispers*. She recounted those four years in more detail. Through a paperback copy, my mom stores her painful memories of loss and hardship. She held steadfast in her belief that my father's spirit had guided us to safety. I hope to relieve my pain on paper as well. My memories were from my nine-year-old perspectives and the punishment I experienced away from Mom.

Chapter Three
Retribution

The Real Hunger Games

I remember when we finally settled in a remote area. It was in the province of Pursat. Apparently, Pursat became the deadliest destination under the Khmer Rouge.

Mom and Dad did not know what to expect as we were settling, waiting for the real destination. The game of purging began via volunteering to disclose our biographies.

Somehow, city dwellers like us were viewed as criminals. We were branded as corrupt and traitors. How was it possible? We were the working class in the city. How could anyone believe that everyone in Phnom Penh was corrupt and a traitor? No matter what we said, it was a fact that we came from Phnom Penh; we deserved the punishment without committing the crime.

At the processing center, Mom and Dad reported four children. We were assigned a shed for all of us. It was nothing elaborate. It was at least a sleeping area off the ground, and a roof covered with hay and bamboo shoots. It was a nicer cottage than the one I used to see when Dad took us to the countryside for a picnic and camping.

However, everything about the Khmer Rouge action was brutal and mysterious. We were stripped of any belongings that were deemed self-sufficient, such as pots and pans. There was no need for other materials other than the clothes we had on. There was no blanket, no pillow, no towels, no personal essentials, no hygiene products. We were to live like animals.

Our family was separated into different groups. Dad had to report to the men's group early each morning, while Mom joined the women's group. All the children, including my siblings and me, were sent to the children's pavilion. There, we were sorted based on our age and height to determine the type of work we were assigned. I was taken away for labor, likely because I appeared older. As for my three brothers, I couldn't remember what tasks the Khmer Rouge assigned them.

There were no playgrounds. There were tasks to be completed. At first, the job was light. I was told to stack up freshly cut wood in the community kitchen. It seemed like I was moving items from one place to another without any purpose but to exhaust the energy that I still possessed.

Afterward, I was allowed to return to the shed, where I was glad to see my three brothers there. In the evening, we saw our parents return from their duties. They were both exhausted.

We were looking forward to the community dining. It was supposed to be the meal that rewarded us for contributing to the state. We were constantly hungry because we had no way to provide for ourselves. Every resource was controlled by the State, leaving us entirely dependent on those in charge of distributing food.

I was excited to head to the community dining hall. After a day of activities, my body needed refreshment. I had no idea what it was like to eat with other people other than my own family members. I thought about the environment that had a sense of countryside living. At the same time, I felt a sense of fear and secretiveness.

Perhaps I was just trying to adapt to an unfamiliar environment. I felt that as the oldest child at that moment, I was obligated to assist my younger brothers to feel comfortable in the environment and ease the concerns of my parents. Somehow, they still worried about us.

At the communal dining space, we were not allowed to stay together as a family. The adults were directed into one section. The women and men were seated separated. I could not see my parents from a distance.

My brothers and I were directed to the children's group. We were assigned to a group with other kids. My group consisted of children of various ages and sizes, from older and bigger kids to younger ones. There were about ten of us in total. I was glad that I was with my brothers. Among us were three Chinese Cambodian boys who appeared larger than we were and had lighter skin. There were about three younger boys of Phirum's age as well.

No adult was guiding us in this community dining ground. At least, we were given a coconut bowl each. All of us were hungry. I was expecting a bowl of rice and a main course to share evenly in the group. Yet, there was only one large bowl with rice porridge. The minute that bowl was placed on the ground the bigger kids fought to grab and slurp without knowing whether it was hot or cold. It was like the rest of us did not exist. Those who reached the rice bowl were able to get some.

I was confused. It happened so fast. I did not understand how communal eating worked. The younger kids and I did not get anything. My brother, Baron, was able to snatch the big bowl for a slurp before the big kids took it back. It was back and forth among kids who were willing to push each other for the food. I could only watch helplessly. I was not aware that there were children who had to fight for food. It was like they knew how to be quick and brutal for the purpose of self-preservation. I was taught to have table manner and to consider others. It was the first time that I formed my bias opinion toward Cambodian Chinese kids.

Apparently, my brothers and I lack primitive behaviors to fend for ourselves. We were not raised to be selfish. We were not prepared that we had to fight for our share. We were considered weak. The stronger ones would survive. The weaker ones would die. The elimination process was based on animal instinct: self-preservation.

I did not understand the intention of the revolution at the time. I just knew the selfish kids as "Kone Ott-Pugh" (a kid with no manners). I referred to them quietly. It was about survival, and I did not understand the situation that I was in. I was supposed to fight for the right to live with food. I felt betrayed by my parents for teaching me civility and consideration for others.

My brothers and I were disheartened when we received no food. As we returned to our shelter, we realized our lack of preparation and did not anticipate the need to compete for food. Despite our hunger, we chose not to burden our parents with our situation. To cope, we drank water to suppress our hunger and reminisced about the meals from our past, regretting any food we had previously wasted. We promised that, if given another chance, we would never take food for granted again.

We even recalled how we loved French Bread with condensed milk. Mom would buy two baguettes each morning. She would cut it evenly into six-inch pieces. We would take one each. Sometimes, I would make hot milk using condensed milk to dip the bread. Sometimes, I would just dip my bread directly into condensed milk.

Each morning, we took turns stopping the boy on a bicycle carrying a tall bamboo basket holding the freshly baked bread. He would yell, "Hot Bread is coming," loud enough for the entire neighborhood to hear. It was right outside our front door. It was kind of fun before everything changed so quickly. We were now starving and could only imagine the food we used to eat in the morning and night.

Baron was often late to the breakfast table. He would argue with Mom that her measurements were not equal. He assumed that the last person would get the smaller piece.

Mom cut it according to how the bread was made sometimes. She gave the beginning and the end of the two-foot-long bread a bit longer because it was skinnier and harder at the edges. The middle part had more meat, and it was thicker inside. Baron took one look and immediately felt the decision was unfair. He argued with Mom about it, but she had enough. To settle the issue, she told him that if he wanted a better choice, he needed to be the first one at the table next time. He took her advice, making sure to arrive early each morning. With the chance to pick his favorite piece of bread, he was finally satisfied. We laughed at how ridiculous it was to give our mom a tough time over the bread. Sometimes, Baron did not even finish his piece after making all the fuss about who might get the bigger piece. However, for him, it was about making his own choice. He did not like it when Mom and Dad chose one for him. We reminisced about other foods that we disliked. If we could go back to the day when we could eat nutritious meals, we would never complain again. We promised to change our behaviors over food when our stomachs were emptied.

We quietly settled into our sleeping area, attempting to sleep despite our hunger. On a positive note, the lack of basic hygiene supplies meant our parents did not need to remind us about brushing our teeth before bed. In retrospect, their primary concern was our future, which filled them with greater fear.

The following day, my brother Baron devised a plan to ensure equitable food distribution among the children. He brought a stick to the communal dining area and used it to prevent the older, more aggressive children from taking the rice porridge before others had a chance. Baron instructed everyone to place their coconut shell bowls around the main bowl and then carefully portioned the porridge evenly. He made sure every child got their share, earning respect for his fair leadership.

I was proud of my younger brother, Baron. It was like he bloomed in adversity. He knew how to solve problems. He knew how to take care of others. He knew how to survive in the situation we were in. Unlike me, I was still in shock at what was going on. I was confused. I did not accept the situation that I was in. How was it possible that the government attempted to starve the children? How was it possible that we were not allowed to go back home? I was waiting for a miracle to get me through the tough time.

Baron left such an impression on me from that day. The next day, he delegated the scooping duty to another kid as he sat protecting the bowl to allow fair distribution to all the kids in our group.

If children were the future of the revolution, why did they starve us? It was clear that the revolution intended to eliminate certain groups of people and their children. It was a grudge against city dwellers, educators, ethnics minorities, and social and cultural fabric of the twentieth century in Cambodia. To act on those biases to justify eliminating corruption was such a stretch of the imagination.

We were playing a game of survival in which the old people were against the new people. It was the rural population versus the city dwellers. If the setting was in rural and jungle areas, the advantage certainly went to the rural population. It was no longer just about working hard to earn a daily portion of food. Survival now depends on knowing how to use plants and animals to strengthen our immune systems against exhaustion caused by malnutrition. I remember a time when I worked alongside a group of kids my age. During a break, we spotted a fruit tree nearby. Hunger led us to believe the fruit was safe. The fruit was similar to a cherry, but smaller and red. I tasted one at first cautiously. Several children consumed a portion directly from their hands. I noticed the sweet taste at first, then it was bitter with acid cutting through my tongue. I spit out immediately. The tongue appeared to be bleeding, while some children expressed their discomfort vocally. We abandoned the tree. From that time, I learned to control my hunger.

Unfortunately, my youngest brother was showing signs of starvation. His body was declining. It was unusual for me to see the Khmer Rouge adults do nothing to save children who had the same condition as my brother.

All I understood at the time was that the Khmer Rouge people hated people like me, coming from the city, regardless of how old we were. What I did not comprehend was why we were enemies when we were just children who happened to be born in Phnom Penh.

Tragedy Strikes

We made it to 1976. Mom and Dad did everything they could with what they had to prolong our lives. Mom did what she could to keep the four of us together in our shed as stricter rules were enforced on us new people.

Dad was now separated from us and moved to the men's group. We did not get to see him every night anymore. Mom was ordered to work out in the fields regularly. I was at work near our camp so that I could watch my younger brothers.

As the eldest daughter, my mother was instructed in various skills to support her family of ten children. Sewing was one of the skills she perfected. It became handy when she could alter black uniforms for the leaders of her women's group. She thereby earned enough social capital to allow us children to remain with her. Still, each of us had to perform duties around the camp to earn the minimum portion of our daily nutrients.

Unfortunately, my youngest brother, Phirum, who was six years old, became ill. His body was malnourished, and he quickly took a turn for the worse. His tiny body became skin and bones. I could count the small ribs that were displayed for me to see.

Mom did what she could for him. Without food or medicine, she was completely helpless. Watching her own child waste away, unable to do anything to save him, was pure torture. His body grew weaker by the minute, yet his spirit remained unbroken. Every so often, he managed a faint smile at me and my two brothers, reassuring us not to worry, almost as if he had already accepted that death was unavoidable. He made it seem effortless to die of hunger.

He began to close his eyes slowly as he was about to go to sleep. There was no more movement that I could see. I watched him slowly telling his brain to shut off one cell at a time. As the end came near, he gasped for air one last time before his body became so still. I was charged with watching him. It was time for me to find Mom.

I did not cry until I saw Mom cry. Then, we all cried. It was only when Phirum's body was moved to a grave behind the camp in the jungle that I realized he had passed away. Mom would justify that it was better for him to die than to suffer longer. To me, I was not accepting the relief of suffering without a reason. It was cruel enough to deprive children of proper nutrition to survive. I did not understand how any adult would allow this to happen to children. I began to see the dark side of my people. I began to question why I was taught to be kind and compassionate when I witnessed the adults looking away when children needed their help. What did we do to deserve such treatment?

A week later, my other brother Varin became ill as well. His body showed no sign of recovery. Soon, he was no longer able to move. When Mom touched his skin, it turned red. It was weird. The skin and bone began to change color. We had no idea what kind of disease he picked up from our unhealthy environment with no food or clean water. In this environment, eventually, the body would give out. Depriving children of food is considered more harmful than physical punishment.

My brother Varin was eight with OCD, yet he managed to survive for months. He changed the way he was to avoid making our parents worry about him. To me, he was the most unselfish son.

During the chaotic evacuation from our home, Varin was calm and collected. He refused to add any special preference to his daily routine. He seemed to grasp our situation. It was crucial to him that we remained united. Never mind, we slept on the ground. We ate with our hands instead of utensils. We had no essentials for our hygiene. We had no toothbrushes, soap, or extra clothes. We did not complain. We accepted the conditions that were imposed by the government. At least, we made it through 1975.

By 1976, Varin's body could no longer endure relentless suffering. There was no defense to any disease when the body endured months of malnutrition. In his final days, he experienced severe hunger. At last, he turned to Mom, pleading for anything to satisfy one final craving. When starvation became unbearable, we would find comfort in reminiscing about the meals Mom used to cook. Although it was not a frequent occurrence, dining with Lok Lack—stir-fried beef served atop a bed of lettuce, tomatoes, and onions, accompanied by a lemon, pepper, and salt sauce—was an exceptional experience. It was simple yet elegant. It was considered a delicacy. Mom did what she could for him. She found a few roasted rat legs. I had no idea where she got them. Varen was in heaven. He thought they were chicken. He had to convince himself it was chicken.

The rat's leg reminded me of my dad. It was the beginning of the Khmer Rouge when rule was not as strict. Both men and women could obtain food by gathering or trading valuables. It was one evening. Daylight revealed a barren countryside, marked only by rice paddies and a few trees. Everyone finished their meal, but the amount served was insufficient. I could not recall what we were doing exactly, but dad was surrounded by other men. Suddenly, a rat the size of a squirrel came from nowhere, daring to appear before a group of hungry men. Dad and all the men stood up quickly, chasing the rat as if their survival depended on it. I watched with embarrassment. I saw the desperation on my father's face. He knew he did not have the strength to catch what he thought might give his four children some nutrient. Nevertheless, he gave it a try. He came back tired and empty-handed. He looked as though he failed us. He was disappointed. Dad was not made to chase rodents for food. He worked in an office environment and wore a suit and tie. Dad had never experienced starvation before. Suddenly, he had nothing. He could not support and care for his own family. He was at the mercy of the revolution. He was told when to work, what to eat, how much he could eat, and where he could not go. It was an imprisonment in the countryside without any rights.

As I felt sad remembering that moment under the Khmer Rouge I recalled a great time I had with Dad prior to the Khmer Rouge as well. It was some Sunday mornings when dad took us to have Noodle Soup. It was the moment that I felt like I was a kid. The Khmer Rouge never allowed me to be just a kid. What kind of government was it to starve children to death? We were not allowed to find our own food when water was filled with fish, when nature gave us a bundle of nutrients.

Varin requested chicken meat from Mom before he died. He craved protein. It had been months since we had been deprived of food. Mom did what she could. Somehow, she got him a rat's leg. She gave it to him to eat. Varen was already hallucinating. He chewed on it as though it were a chicken leg in a smaller size. He looked satisfied. His condition had no chance without treatment. He endured the pain in his body until he took his last breath.

Mom held her breath long enough. When she sobbed quietly, I knew then that Varen was gone. I only paid attention to how horrible his body looked. I saw a lifeless body that did not seem significant to anyone else except for Mom, Baron, and me. Dad was not with us. He probably could not bear to see his clean, proper, and always dignified son die this way. It seemed like last week when I watched Phirum's lifeless body. It was too soon for me to witness another brother's death.

Mom tried to hold everything together because of Baron and me. She sent words to Dad about the loss of Phirum, but she did not get to send words to him about Varin. She even wondered if they, the Khmer Rouge leader of his group, felt compassion enough to allow Dad to even come back to us for a visit. It had been so long since we saw Dad.

It was weeks after Varin died when Dad appeared at our camp. Apparently, he begged for permission to visit when Phirum died. It was shocking to him to realize that Varin also died by the time he was allowed to visit before nightfall, where he would have to leave right back at dawn.

Seeing him after months of absence visually and in communication was a boost to my mental and emotional health. Somehow, it gave me the strength to endure another grueling day without proper nutrition. Baron and I were overwhelmed with gratitude. Although I was depressed to see the change in his physical health. He was not the father that I used to know. He was a lifeless old man.

Regardless of his appearance, Mom threw herself at him in disbelief. He came. He knew with his eyes wandering around our shed for another child. There were no words. The silence was so intense that even the sound of a pin dropping would have been so loud. The four of us sat in unbearable stillness. I felt torn about keeping our family together, knowing deep down that there was no future in my father's eyes. In that moment, the only thing he could offer us was one final embrace. The warmth of our shared love was the only comfort we had left. We all sobbed together quietly in our ways, knowing that what was to come was not an easy journey for us.

I was still shocked about his appearance. I could count his rib cage. His hair was all gray. What had he been doing for the Angka? What kind of punishment did he receive for being a man from the city? He did say that he was a Taxi driver. Wasn't that enough to persecute him less? My father used to look sharp in a white-collar shirt and tie. He was the typical office-suit kind of guy. What did they do to him? His ripped short pants barely covered his knees. Not to mention, it was ripped front and back. He was barely walking straight. His legs had no strength. There were signs of overwork and nutrient deficiency. I did not understand what caused a country to significantly change the life of an ordinary family man. The man that I remember was full of life. By nature, Dad was a man with social skills. He was well dressed, well liked, well respected by his peers, and well groomed. Within months, he became disoriented. Perhaps it was intentional to break a man by taking away his family, dignity, and pride.

While we were forbidden to express our emotions or display any affection where the Khmer Rouge members could see us, our eyes said it all. Dad was more emotional than Mom. His tears spoke for him. Baron and I were thrilled to see him after months of not knowing his whereabout. Once the sun completely disappeared, darkness consumed the campground and our shed. We could no longer see the expression instead of words. My father endeavored to discreetly share his last thoughts before departing for his camp at dawn. The permission to visit was barely twenty-four hours.

"Look out for each other." I heard softly.

Dad wanted to give us hope. He forced himself to believe we would go back to the day where we could live our lives as before. However, we had to survive this inhumane treatment first. The only thought that came to my mind about liberation was food. The freedom to find the food and eat it without being restricted as though we did not deserve to eat to live. We could finally eat again. The mere thought of food brought a smile to my face.

Unfortunately, it was the last time I ever saw my dad alive. Mom said that her group leader would not disclose the information of his death until months later. He might be even death shortly after visiting us for one last time.

My Brother, The Hero

Several months later, Baron and I were relocated to another village. We were not allowed to stay with Mom. She claimed that we were too small to be sent to the children's camp. Instead, she asked to have us settled where there were villages with mostly elders.

Somehow, Mom knew that my paternal grandparents would be there. They were able to look out for Baron and me. Mom used her tailor skills to earn favors among her group leaders to get us sent to the village. I was thrilled to be around my family.

My enthusiasm diminished when Grandma did not allow my brother and me to share the sleeping quarters off the ground. She claimed there was not enough space. She had to watch two of my cousins as well. They were about four and six years old. However, there was enough space to sleep away from danger. She did not care about our safety. She was determined to harbor her dislike for our mother. She forgot that we were her grandchildren as well. I was disappointed that Grandfather did not defend us regarding Grandmother's judgment. He saw no use in being on her bad side when the condition of our environment was difficult enough. At least, he got satisfaction by having us near him. At the same time, we were more fortunate to be sent there than anywhere else.

However, Grandma never forgot her disapproval of Mom. She blamed Mom for bewitching Dad. It was because of Mom that dad failed to select the wife that she thought would bring more benefit to the family.

Grandmother was so influenced by status and material possessions that she forgot about the happiness of her son. Somehow, her hatred transferred from Mom to us, her own grandchildren. On the other hand, Grandfather Pol was a saint. He was kind and generous and supported his son one hundred percent. I also learned that grandmother did not come to Mom and Dad's wedding. I found out from extended relatives rather than from Mom. Because Mom would never say anything bad about my paternal grandparents, I could only wonder, even when we lost everything, how grandmother could still harbor the hatred.

Baron would not hear of unequal treatment. He gave grandmother a week to realize her actions. She failed to be fair. Baron took the issue to the authority, the Khmer Rouge section leader.

Bravely, he asked if we could have our meal portion given to us directly, separating from our grandparents and the two toddlers.

"Why?" the leader asked.

"I am bigger now. I do not want to be a burden to her. She has other responsibility."

I was mesmerized by my brother's logical explanation. I was amazed at his ability to communicate without giving away the differentiated treatment that his grandmother gave us. He was poised to seek fairness without putting down others to do so. I was even more grateful to him when the leader agreed. I was over the moon. We would finish our portion at the community hall before going back to sleep underneath the wooden cottage.

Since then, I have followed my brother everywhere I could. Sometimes, I was sent to work with elders doing manual laundry for the Khmer Rouge leaders. We had to contribute to the labor force by doing a variety of work in support of the main productive forces out on the field, the adults.

Grandmother never spoke to us again, but Grandfather was different. Every time he saw us, he greeted us with a gentle smile, filled with quiet pride. Though his health was failing, he still pushed himself to complete his daily chores as best he could. But when I looked closely, I could see the exhaustion in his eyes, the weight of his thoughts. I had no doubt he thought about his sons every single day. He knew that he had lost two grandsons already. It was a matter of time before he heard about the fate of his children. I wondered what he thought about the revolution. He was in his seventies. He was supposed to retire to a peaceful life, yet he was isolated to a small camp where he had to work to receive his daily portion. More importantly he was cut off from the outside world and the whereabout of his families. He used to be in law enforcement. He used to know what to do to keep people safe. Now he was helpless, waiting for the day of his demise. He saw injustice under the Khmer Rouge but couldn't act. He did not speak about his past due to concerns about possible repercussions for his family.

Sleeping on the ground over a stack of hay was not comfortable or safe. Sometimes, it was cold. Sometimes, it gets wet. Baron and I managed to stay for months. Even with the daily portion of rice porridge, it was still not enough to complete the nutrients needed for us to function without being hungry. Baron became an expert at catching insects. He would find a way to roast crickets, grasshoppers, and even geckos. He shared that extra protein with me.

One night, I felt something bite me. The pain around my ankle was sharp. I could not move my right leg afterward. Somehow, I was able to tolerate the pain until morning. When morning came, Baron caught a scorpion. He insisted it was the culprit that had harmed me. The scorpion became his extra nutrient.

I was still unable to move my leg. Baron told grandfather. He arrived promptly to examine the injury. He saw how swollen my ankle was. He promptly sought authorization to search for natural herbs. He also reported my injury so that I would not get punished for not reporting to work. Baron left me to grandfather. He had to report for work.

Grandfather returned with many green leaves. I had no idea what they were. It could be turmeric or galanga leaves. Herbs were commonly used for cooking and pain relief. He roasted one of them slightly and wrapped it around my wound. It was soothing. Somehow, it numbed the pain in that area. I was able to bear the pain when he suddenly squeezed out the poison, he said. Subsequently, he masticated additional leaves and applied the resulting substance onto the wound. He roasted more leaves to cover the infected area, just like a bandage. Somehow, the natural remedy gave me a sense of tranquility. I fell asleep without being aware of my condition. When I opened my eyes, I saw Grandfather Pol was very attentive to me. He gave me water to drink. For the first time, I saw a humble and gentle man. Did he really feel sorry for me? Perhaps he was. Perhaps it hurts him more to know that he has already lost two grandsons. He had no idea where all his five adult sons were.

Grandfather was a retired security officer at the rubber plantation. He worked for the French. He protected the giant corporation at that time. I wondered who. Why was there such a need to secure and protect revenues that were to be shipped off to a foreign country without the benefit of the people who worked and lived to make the revenues?

Would this contribute to how the Khmer Rouge hated the French so much? It was not just corruption. It was a plain robbery of a small country with natural resources in soil and in nature. What were the people of the past thinking? Was it the reason the French appointed Prince Sihanouk at the age of nineteen, a spoiled, privileged kid who was supposed to have a bloodline from the great leaders of the past like Jayvaraman II?

Regardless, I was sure that if time allowed, my grandfather would do more to ensure that my generation would not suffer as I do now. Was he disappointed or regretful that he did not do more during his time as an adult? Would anyone ever expect that the Khmer Rouge was going to do what they were doing?

Judging from his expression of sadness, I thought he would. He never thought about losing his sons and grandsons to such an extremist group.

He was in his seventies. He was expected to take pleasure in spending time with his grandchildren. He was supposed to travel around the country. Instead, he tried to save his only granddaughter from dying due to poisonous wildlife. At least, I have a great memory of my paternal grandfather. The warmth and caring he showed me was enough for me to forgive my paternal grandmother for mistreatment. After all, she believed that wealth and status were more important than emotions.

Eventually, I was able to walk. However, I began to have a regular fever and chill every day at the same time. I began to tremble as the fever grew. It started with a chill from my spine. Then, it erupted into a seismic shake. Baron would sit on me sometimes to control the movement. I felt very cold as well. Grandfather would find things to cover me with, including hay. The effect happened every afternoon. It took at least one hour. When the fever broke, the shaking stopped as well. Afterward, I would get so hungry. Mom called it malaria.

Fortunately, grandfather requested our transfer. He added that we were old enough to be at the camp where Mom was assigned. Because of my condition, Mom would be suited to care for me after her work. It was the best that grandfather could do to avoid being mistreated by our grandmother.

Our wish was granted. Mom was allowed to pick us up from the elder and children's camp. There was a sense of relief in the eyes of my paternal Grandfather as we said "goodbye." I did not imagine that I would never see him again.

Mom said that he died shortly after we left. Grandmother died shortly after Grandfather. My young cousins returned to their mom.

During the walk back to Mom's camp, I had my daily episode of malaria attack, the shakes, and fever. Mom had to stop under a tree for me to endure my hour-long chill and fever.

Afterward, Mom gave me mango, and it was like heaven.

"Sweet and juicy," I said aloud. I had no idea how she was able to obtain the fruit. I was glad to have something to fill my stomach after the fever and chills. I was exhausted.

We kept on walking. We were halted on multiple occasions by the Khmer Rouge guards. Mom had to show her permission paper to continue.

The malaria did not go away. In the morning, I worked in the camp with Baron; in the afternoon, I returned to our hut feeling chills and fever. Mom had to work all day. We did not see her much during the daytime, but we saw her at night. The comfort of being in the same tent was enough for us.

As I was struggling with malaria, Baron was struggling with malnutrition. His body began to bloat so badly that he could no longer walk. Being still was never his strong suit. He was an active child. Just like Dad, he was friendly to everyone. He was easy to talk to. I was his older sister, yet he took care of me better than I took care of him. He would always share his extra crickets or grasshoppers with me.

I recalled our stay at the village where we were placed with our paternal grandparents. Baron came across a Khmer Rouge leader smoking a cigarette. Without fearing the man, he admired the long blow of smoke that came out from his mouth. The man almost finished with the cigarette, judging from how short it got.

"Are you throwing away the butt of it?" Baron asked.

"Yes," the man answered. Before he could flick it to the ground, Baron asked.

"May I, have it?"

"Why?"

"Maybe my grandfather can smell the nicotine, even if he cannot smoke." I was scared on behalf of Baron at his outrageous request. It was like he forgot that we were in danger because we were not the "old people." We were not a protective class. We were the enemy just because we were born in the city.

I remembered the biggest smile on my grandfather's face when Baron gave him the cigarette butt. Whatever worry he had, it suddenly disappeared at that moment. He pretended to enjoy the cigarette as though he was smoking for hours. Baron took the time to extend the lifeline for his grandfather, who did not care about himself at all. Now, his body began to show signs of deterioration. It was bloated before, and it was deflated. The liquid discharged in the form of diarrhea began to leave his body slowly. He was terribly weak. He found the energy to ask Mom for a spoonful of rice porridge. I could not bear to see how horrible he would feel on the inside. Baron fought to stay alive if any adults had any conscience to save him.

Unfortunately, Mom could not find anything that would allow her to gain access to a spoonful of rice porridge. She was willing to work overtime if it meant earning extra food for her child. It was forbidden. I would have done the same if I could have gotten something to help my brother stay alive. We followed the rules. We could not steal or beg. Mom had been warned that the government would not waste any food on sick individuals. I thought the cruelest thing to do to children was to deprive them of food. They died because their bodies had no proper nutrition to build an Immune System to defend themselves from any bad bacteria. I hated this Angka. I also hated the adults, especially the Khmer Rouge leaders, especially the adult women who were privileged because they were the previous peasants, because they hated people who were exposed to city living, even children. How was that possible? My brother Baron never did anything bad except to stand up for the weaker one like me. I did not understand what possessed the Khmer Rouge supporters to turn evil.

That night, it was chilly. The air was cooler than any other night. We had limited clothing and blankets. Whatever we had, Mom used it all to keep us warm. We kept each other warm by sleeping remarkably close to one another. Baron slept in the middle. Mom and I were on each side of him. I did not care if I smelled his excrement. Mom fell asleep first. I was trying to stay up waiting for him because he seemed weaker than usual. He seemed to ask for water often. At one point, I noticed Baron chewing in his sleep, his mouth moving as if he were enjoying the French bread with con-densed milk we used to enjoy. When he swallowed water, his expression suggested he was tasting a spoonful of rice and meat. His favorite dish had always been Lok Lak. Lok Lak is a stir-fried beef over a bed of lettuce, tomatoes, and onion, topped with lemon, salt, and pepper. I am sure he was hallucinating about food at the time. He did say something that I could not understand. I did not know when I fell asleep.

When I opened my eyes, it was already bright. The morning had arrived. I was relieved. It would be easier for me to help Baron with what he needed. I was willing to give my food ratio for the day if it meant to make him better. I knew he was asking for rice at night. Mom could not find any. According to Angka, if one could not work, one did not deserve to eat. I was ready to work that morning.

Baron was still asleep. He was on his side, turning away from me. I could not leave him without first checking on how he was doing.

"It's morning," I said enthusiastically. Baron loved mornings. He was always looking forward to a new day, regardless of the circumstances we were in. To him, each morning offered a new opportunity. Perhaps it was hope that gave him energy. Unlike me, I was angry at the situation we were in, because there was no explanation as to why. Even though I was a child, I deserved to know why. Baron wanted to live so much. There was a fighting spirit in him. I did not think I had what he had.

Tragically, fate was not kind to him. His body could no longer carry his spirit. There was no sunlight that morning. There was stillness in the air. I saw no movement.

Baron lied there face up. I saw ants roaming on his frail face. How dare they? Even insects had no mercy on a little boy. I froze at that moment. I did not know what to do. Then I realized that I needed to find Mom.

I did not need the adult to confirm to me that my brother had died. I needed to tell Mom that we had just lost a great one. I was shocked, anger, sadness, and resentment when I ran to fetch Mom. I was still confused and did not understand how it all happened. How could adults be so cruel, especially the one who stole the cup of rice that Mom had traded to save Baron?

It had been years since we were in this terrible condition. I never ran the way I ran to look for Mom. I ran as though I was angry at the world. I ran as though I wanted to drop death as well. Tears ran down my face as I kept on running through the sidewalk of a rice paddy.

Finally, I located Mom in the rice field, where she was working with a group of women. When she saw me, she immediately asked permission to leave. She knew it was about Baron.

As we walked back to the shed, each step got more heavier. I walked behind Mom quietly without making a sound or uttering a word. Mom walked faster than I expected. I felt that no matter how difficult I experienced taking each step, my will could take me back to Baron.

Without hesitation, Mom hurried toward Baron once we reached our shed. I fell on my knees next to Mom. Immediately, she gathered the tiny body in her arms. I watched her intently, as if freezing at this moment in time. For the first time, I fully grasped that the vibrant, charismatic, and fearless boy I once knew as my brother was gone. In death, he looked nothing like himself, his body, frail and abused, reduced to nothing but skin and bone. Yet, despite everything, I was in awe of how much he had grown through hardship. When Phirum and Varen died, I was sad, but I did not feel anguish about life. The demise of Baron left a huge hole in my heart. Perhaps I was selfish because I thought of being alone. I had no one to look out for me. There was no longer anyone to provide me with additional proteins from crickets and grasshoppers. I had no one to reminisce about the time we had French bread.

Initially, my mother exhibited a minimal emotional response. She appeared to be in a daze of a bad dream. Perhaps, she told herself, it was not real. She could not lose three sons and a husband in less than a year. At that moment, she closed her eyes and reopened them again. She realized it was not a dream. She lost her child once again. Suddenly, tears were filling her eyes. When it finally rolled over her cheeks, it was like a stream washing over her face. I did not catch what else she was saying except to hear about the end of his suffering. It was like she was relieved that he departed from us. There was no more suffering for him. He entered a better place now.

While mom convinced herself that my brother had found solitude in heaven, I was consumed by confusion and sadness. I could not stop my tears from rolling down my cheeks. At the same time, I was bitter to have to witness his passing and the condition that he was in. Besides realizing that I would be all alone to navigate the challenges of the senseless revolution that viewed a kid like me as the enemy, I wanted to be in a "better place" like Baron, too. Would my turn come sooner? Would Mom have to bid farewell and say that I would be in a better place as well?

I could not accept how my brothers died, especially Baron. He fought so hard to beat the odds of dying. Yet, fate was so cruel to him. It was inhumane the way the adults treated us children. I despised the woman who stole that cup of rice from Mom with the trade. Ultimately, I cried because I lost my hero brother.

Mom cried until there were no more tears. She carefully wrapped her last son's body in whatever material she had left that belonged to her. She was careful to give her last son a piece of what she had made so he would remember her. She asked me to say goodbye, but I was too emotional to even look at his lifeless body. I helped Mom carry Baron's body to the grave site.

Two Men were assisting us in digging Baron's grave. Baron's body was so thin and small. The men barely dug the grave deep enough to cover the body. The hole was not suitable to prevent wild animals from getting to the bones. It was not deep enough to secure a burial site. I noticed the same way with my other two brothers. Somehow, a body was not necessarily important to maintain. It was the way of the Angka. Perhaps, we were lucky to even allow the burial. After all, the Angka took death as nonproductive activities to concern oneself. The task was completed promptly by the two men, who then returned to their station. Mom and I were left to say our farewells before she had to report back for duties. It was just me now. I had no idea what went through her mind. Was she contemplating what to do with me? How would she protect me? What was to become of me? Mom had her moment of silence as I remained frozen. I did not feel anything at that moment.

At the very least, my presence gave her a reason to hold on. She needed to stay strong for me. There was no time to grieve, if she allowed herself to dwell on the pain of losing her husband and three sons, the weight of it might break her. The sorrow could be so overwhelming that even breathing would become unbearable. However, knowing that I was still in danger, Mom needed to continue living life with suffering. She comforted herself by believing in Buddha. This was the end-of-life suffering for Baron. Mom prayed that Baron would join Dad, Phirum, and Varin in the afterlife.

That night, we slept in silence, numbed by the emotional cruelty of the revolution. My brothers could have lived with basic nutrition. They would have worked hard to earn it.

I was still processing the fact that I was now alone. The noise of living with four siblings was now complete silence. What would I go back home to if, by miracle, we got to go back to Phnom Penh? My thoughts went wild. I felt angry at what had transpired. I did not understand the purpose of the revolution. I did not understand why adults had no compassion toward children. Why? Not even Mom could explain to me why. What constitutes just cause?

According to my mom's justification in Buddhism, my brothers were now free from suffering. Nonetheless, I did not approve of how they died. Suppose Buddha intended to save them from life suffering; why did Buddha allow them to suffer before they died? It was how they died that left such a traumatic scar in my heart.

When Mom told me about my dad's death, I could not help but see how horrible his body looked when I last saw him. I felt sad when I remembered my brother Varin, who, in his final days, chewed on a small rat's leg, believing it was chicken. Then there was Baron, who, on the night he died, pretended to eat imaginary food, trying to satisfy a hunger that could never be filled. If there were just a spoon of rice porridge that night, he would live to see sunlight the next day.

I was angry. I was hopeless. I wanted to join them as well. I knew that my turn would soon come. I just did not know when and how.

I was barely a decade old, and I felt like I was ready to quit life. What else awaited me besides labor? Mom was right; the end of life would be the end of suffering. I wanted the end of life-suffering. It was too much for me to endure the loss of my brothers. It would be different if I did not have to witness how they died. Now that I did, it was difficult to erase the images of what adults did to young children. There was no reason to condemn them in that way. Nothing made sense to me.

Children Labor Camps

I was allowed to stay and work with Mom for about three months after Baron passed. I worked as an adult at eleven years old. I earned the same ratio of food as my mom. We shared the bitterness of what we encountered in those months.

It was not long before Mom was selected to move forward with the women's group. What was left of this camp were older women and children. I was left behind as Mom moved out. She said goodbye. Trying to tell me about a zillion times how to take care of myself.

"I already knew how," I replied. There was nothing new. I anticipated the cruelty of this "Angka" that adults referred to when it came to the policies. At one point, Mom requested that I stay with her, stating that I was capable of handling an adult's task. It was no use.

"Everyone has to do what Angka said." Mom's leader responded.

I wondered what Angka looked like. This Angka had so much power over people. I wished to see the face of Angka, who enforced such strict regulations. How could Angka not see the suffering of its people?

Mom was sad to leave me. But she had no choice. Angka was now testing Mom's mental strength. She would break eventually when everyone in her family perished one by one. Angka planned to detach the emotional and psychological connection between family members.

As mom's group marched out on foot at dawn, I was also up to take my daily assignment. They moved me closer to other kids. I guessed it would be easier to control the guard if we were all in one place. I carried the bamboo sleeping mat that Mom gave me. I could sleep on any surface: dirt, wood, hay, whatever. I was no longer scared of what was going to happen to me. I tried to be responsible when my brothers were around. It seemed like there was no point for me to be good anymore. At the same time, I did not go out of my way to rise against the revolution. I was only a kid. I was waiting for the end-of-life suffering.

It had been months since Mom was gone. The children and adults seemed to be fewer than I recognized. The work that they had me do seems to be double. They were always plowing the field for a new garden. Sometimes, I was instructed to dig. Was I digging for graves? I did not recall. I did everything that I was told so that I got my daily ratio, then went to rest. It was like clockwork. My mind and body had become so numb to the routine that I no longer felt pain. Occasionally, a shiver runs down my spine. This may be a residual effect of malaria. When that happened, I would retreat to my corner, curl into the fetal position, and surrender to the symptoms, letting them pass on their own. After at least forty minutes, I would break down into sweat. I need water and nutrition immediately. I learned how to take care of myself.

Suddenly, there was a commotion of the camp being shut down. Mothers were allowed to collect their children. Only those mothers who had children were alive. I was told that Mom would be here to pick me up.

So, I waited. On day one, it seemed like half of the camp's population was gone. I was still waiting.

On day two, I was still waiting. By this time, ninety percent of the previous occupants were relocated. I was still waiting. At this point, I moved to the front of the camp entrance. There was a big tree near the entrance that provided good shade for me. I got up at dawn to wait at the entrance for Mom.

I waited and waited.

The camp was almost empty.

I waited from morning to noon, wondering what would happen to me if Mom had not come. Unpleasant thoughts began to crop up in my mind. What if Mom is dead? If I were the last kid here, perhaps what would Angka do to me? Is Mom free of her life-suffering? A million thoughts came to my head. I did not cry. I was not scared. I continued to sit there patiently.

"Kid, you can't wait here." A voice startled me. I had not heard any footsteps coming in my direction.

It was an older woman. She was probably the last one to leave.

"I'm waiting for Mother," I answered her.

"If she was not here by now, she was probably dead. You can come with me," she offered.

Do I have a choice? I thought not. The word "death" was still lingering in my head. I began to think of that possibility. I remember Mom told Baron and me that Angka did not tell her about our father's death until six months later. What if

Mom died already, and no one cared to tell me about Mom because I was a kid? There was only one reason. If Mom failed to come to fetch according to the allowance of Angka for a mother to see their kids, then Mom would probably die.

I began to wonder what my future would be. I guessed the woman would walk me to the next camp, wherever they allowed a kid like me to be around. I kept going until my body completely shut down.

I struggled to get up. Once I did, I walked slowly as though there was no need to go anywhere. There was no hope in my bones. It was good that the old woman's pace was enough for me to keep up with. Otherwise, I was not able to daydream while walking about what the end of suffering would be like. Would I never feel hungry again? I would not need food to survive.

When we started to walk, the sun was directly on top of me. I was told this was noon. The people in rural countries were very smart. They were able to tell time by just looking at the sun. As we kept on walking, I noticed the sun began to descend. It warned us that hour had passed. We passed some empty camps, but the old woman continued with me.

I was not sure how long we had been walking. I kept up with the old woman's pace well. She rested often. I did not understand why the camp needed to be dispersed. Was it to consolidate the rest of the human cattle?

Suddenly, my legs were numb momentarily. I lost hope. I did not know what to do. Was I supposed to wander from one camp to another until nightfall looking for Mom? Why did the old woman stay with me? Most adults seemed to be gone. Was she obligated to stay with me even though I was not her responsibility? She appeared out of nowhere, guiding me toward the path that fate had chosen for me. It was interesting that I saw the scariest images of the starving bodies of my brothers and father. Yet I had no memory of my own appearance. I only knew that I was still moving, still functioning. What gave me the strength to endure such suffering, I could not say. I only wished I had seen my own reflection during that time. It would be seven years before I finally looked into a mirror, until then, I only knew what others looked like, never myself. When Mom said I was skinny during the Khmer Rouge, I dared not to ask her if she saw my rib cage, as I saw in all my three brothers.

We continued walking. We came across another abandoned camp. The debris from the broken huts was scattered throughout the camp. It seemed like there was no need to reuse the camp for further housing. How convenient it was to have people just evaporate out of thin air. Only the ones who could still perform duty got a chance to relocate to another camp. Those who no longer function would eventually meet with death. Approaching the tents near the camp entrance, I heard someone call my name. The voice was weak, with no pitch. However, the wind seemed to carry the voice in the air. I heard it a couple of times.

Then, I stopped walking. The old woman slowed down as well. My name was called once more.

This time, I looked around at all the open and empty tents. I saw a tent that was further away from the rest. It looked like there was a person there. Something told me to walk toward it. The woman followed me.

"Jeat." It was almost like a whisper. I recognized my nickname. The adults never ever called us by our given name. Each child had to have a pet name for it. My actual name was Socheata. Mom used the middle "j-e-a-t," pronounced "Jeat." It meant nationality. My eyes and ears were searching for the owner of the fading sound. My intuition told me that it was Mom. I had to look for her in this abandoned camp.

Surely enough, I saw a frail, thin woman lying on a bamboo mat on the ground under a bamboo tent. It was Mom. She could not move and had no strength left. But when she heard footsteps nearby, she used all the energy she had left. The ground was covered in dry leaves, and anyone entering the camp had to step on them. She signaled that she was sick and couldn't pick me up when the camp moved. It was interesting. It felt like the wind carried her voice to me. It felt like someone, or something, guided me toward the voice. It was no coincidence. If there was a miracle, I was sure that moment was one of them.

Looking at her condition, she had no strength to make a sound. Once, I went to her side, lifting her face to see me to ensure that it was me. I was still alive. She let out a huge sigh of relief. Then, she failed to come back down to catch a breath.

The old woman did not look happy that she had to escort me out of my old camp. She stared at Mom for a second and took her leave. I did not get to say thank you to her. It was like she had more important things to do than to watch Mom and I reunited in a crisis. At least she appeared from nowhere to guide me to Mom. Again, I did not comprehend how fortunate I was to have an adult who provided such direction during a time of devastation. I guessed I might be pathetic enough that no one could abandon me. The crucial moment was when I found Mom. There was nothing else that mattered. Alive or dead, we were able to see each other.

Mom could not walk. It seemed like her body refused to function as she closed her eyes to rest. I quickly roamed around the empty camp for discarded items. I found a water canteen and an extra Kro-ma (scarf) to keep her warm. I waited for her to get up, but the sun was about to set. Then, a patrol guard warned us to evacuate the camp. Those who couldn't move on their own would be left behind permanently. However, before darkness covered the countryside, the ox cart passed by the camp. Mom felt much better speaking. She begged the guy to give us a ride to the next camp. Looking at her condition, he agreed.

There was enough space for Mom to lie down on the cart. I was barely hanging on in the back. If the cart could go faster, I would fall off frequently. It was also a miracle when I was allowed to stay with Mom for the time being, as we reached the next camp.

Day by day, Mom recovered. She was able to sustain her rice porridge. Her energy seemed to improve gradually. She was able to receive light work in the camp. I was still allowed to be by her side. Somehow, the restriction was less enforced. I was able to pick edible green leaves such as P-Tee. I'm not sure if there is a name in English. However, the taste is a bit similar to spinach. It is particularly good for digestion. If you consume too much of it without protein, it can cause diarrhea. I had the experience.

One evening, the thunder attempted to scare everyone in the countryside. However, I was not the least afraid of thunder and storms on their way. I was more afraid of the Khmer adults during those times. I was afraid of whom to trust, even. Perhaps it was the monsoon season. I was not in school for a while. I did not even know what day of the week it was. Every day was like a game for me, and I wanted to see how long I could last. I expected to disappear like my brothers, but hopefully with less suffering. The camp was silent; no one dared to step outside. The adults were resting after a long day of hard work. Only a few kids like me knew about the tallest, biggest mango tree nearby. There were fruits up top that no one was able to get. We anticipated the fruits to drop with such winds and rain. I did not care about what was going to happen to me as long as I got a taste of the sweet and sour mango.

It was dark. We were under the tree waiting for the sound of newly dropped fruit once the wind swayed the branches and leaves together, making the heavy fruits drop by themselves when it was almost time to pick anyway. When we heard that dunk sound into the bushes and grasses underneath, we ran to comb the area for the making, never knowing what other creatures might come out during the rain or were there to begin with. Somehow, I was not afraid of being bitten by wild creatures.

Fortunately, it was like a blind scavenger hunt. I was able to grab one. It was still raining, and the wind began to slow down. I could not help but take a bite of the mango. It was indeed sweet and sour. It felt like years since I had some mangoes. Chewing with rainwater, I lost the authentic taste of the mango. I decided to stop eating so that I could share with Mom later.

We continued to wait for a while longer. Each of us gathered about four to five mangos. When there was no sign of any more fruit falling, we decided to call it quits.

On the way back to our huts, the Khmer Rouge leader, the camp leader, was conveniently waiting at the intersection of our huts. She confiscated all the mangoes, leaving us one each. It was the one that had bitten it. We were disappointed. At the same time, we were glad that we did not get beaten up because we were not supposed to take anything that belonged to the State, including the wild mango.

At least Mom and I enjoyed that one mango I got. There was enough sugar and vitamin C in the fruit to last us a day of rejuvenation.

Our body recovered. The extra nutrient from Tro Kune (morning glory) gave us extra filling. Tro Kune is a green vegetable that is similar to watercress. It can be eaten raw or cooked like vegetables. Besides the root, you can eat stem and leaves. It is packed with vitamins A, C, K, fiber, iron, and folate. I continue to love this vegetable today. I can make many dishes out of it.

Anyhow, this little green plant sustained our vitality. We were careful not to get caught as we picked some on our way back to our camp to be added to our ratio of rice. Most of the time, we ate it raw. This vegetable can be eaten raw or cooked. Additionally, I was impressed by how adults creatively mixed rice porridge with various vegetables and creatures like snails to enrich its nutrients. It was my first time seeing various types of snails in the farmlands.

Mom said we made it to 1978. It was the monsoon season. I was working side by side with Mom as an adult. However, it was not long before Mom was required to push further into the rural camp. I was then sent to another children's camp. It was another goodbye and another uncertainty of when we would reunite again. Mom gave me a blanket, one set of clothing, a shirt, and pants.

I didn't have the slightest idea of geography. I did not know where I was, but in the confines of the children's labor camp. There were more children than I had seen before. There were also "old people" and children. They had more rights than we, "new people" children.

At this camp, I was treated harshly. The daily task was to measure the feet to plow. We were assigned to a sleeping area with other girls. There was about a foot of distance between each of the girls. While I was sleeping, someone stole the extra clothes that Mom had given me. Eventually, someone cut out the buttons off the shirt I had on.

When daylight came the next morning, I would walk, holding the front of my shirt so that I would not be exposed. I was in a girls' camp. I should not be shy, yet I was. Regardless of how rage-looking the shirt was, I served the purpose of covering the sensitive area. Since my shirt had no buttons to close, I felt exposed. I was at the age where I should have been wearing a training bra, but I didn't have one. The older kids laughed at me. I must have seemed funny to them. But I had no other shirt to wear. My guts were feeling like the girls who were laughing at me were the culprits behind the missing buttons.

During a break, I would walk to the grassy area. There, I found tall grass. I used the nail on my finger to cut the grass. I used a thorn from another flower to poke a hole on the other side of my shirt. Somehow, I was able to tie the shirt together with the grass string. Then, I pretended it was a new fashion. At the same time, I saw our children's group leader had all the buttons on her front shirt. She, too, decorated her shirt to show a new fashion. Although I was confused, suppose the revolution banned all color clothing because it represented the corruption of the minds. Why did she decorate her all-black uniform? We, the new people, were not allowed to wear the black uniform because we did not earn it.

My group leader was not much older than I was. She instigated the bullying. Other "old kids" were there to have some fun with us. I wondered what they heard about children like me. Was I the enemy just because I was born in the city?

If I were slow in doing my assignment, they would come to torment me. They would chant a verse to insult me for not knowing the different types of fish. They were not wrong. I would not know the type of fish because I was born in the city, where I was told to go to school instead of fishing like the country kids had to do to ensure that they would be able to eat every day. I did not mind if it was just teasing, but the act of dehumanizing me was intolerable.

កូនអ្នកអំពេញ សីត្រីលេញអាមចេញឆ្អឹង

"Kon Nak Phnom Peng, See Trey Lench, Porm Jench ChaEng."

The "Old" kids bullied me constantly. It was like I was marked to be punished. I wondered why they hated me. What was my crime? Was it because I was never taught to understand which fish had the most bones?

I was never taught to plow the field. I was doing everything they had me do. What else could I do to make them like me?

I was confused and all alone. The rhyming song described a city child who ate a type of fish *trey lench* and fart out bones. They meant to say that I was dumb to eat the fish with the most bones, and when I emitted gas, the bone came out. Till today, I do not know what *Trey Lench* looks like.

Though amused, I couldn't change that I was unfamiliar with farms or rural areas and knew nothing about fish. The fish with many bones was dangerous to eat, so most people in the countryside avoided it. They couldn't risk choking or getting a bone stuck in their throat. Knowing how to eat it properly was a useful skill, but it wasn't fair to criticize me for not knowing. I bet I knew more bedtime stories than they did anyway. There were many jokes at my expense. I no longer had Baron to protect me. Therefore, I accepted every bashing and humiliation.

It had been months since I was placed in this children's camp. I had not seen Mom or heard from her. I was taught to "depend on oneself" (Klune Thee Penk Klune). I was told that I now belonged to Angka. I had no need for parental guidance.

I was taught to disconnect my emotions from my family. In my case, Mom was the only one left. I was taught not to miss her. I was taught not to rely on her, not even for emotional support.

Why did the Angka teach me to disconnect from my family? Was it because when they died, I would not feel anything? Wasn't it too late when I already saw how my three brothers died? My confusion and anger still existed for Angka. It did not matter what they said, but I knew what they had done was wrong. It was not about teaching us kids to be self-reliant but to detach from reality and the feeling of belonging. It was like teaching us to die. We were just kids. We lost hope at the thought of never seeing our family again.

I did not understand what Angka was thinking. If children were to be the property of the government, shouldn't we be in the protective class? We were the human resources that could produce more revenues for Angka. Yet, we were put to work with limited nutrition, and some of us did not survive. Then, what was the thinking behind the children of the future? We were the backbone of the production lines.

Perhaps any children who were exposed to city living were not to be trusted. Therefore, the treatment of children was at a different level depending on where one evacuated from.

In addition, growing up in the children's camp, I had no proper checkup or advice on what was going on with my teeth. For some reason, my baby teeth did not fall out, and my new teeth grew in the wrong direction. I had one on each side of my upper lip, pointing sideways and hurting the inside of my mouth. If I smiled with all my teeth showing, it would look like I had fangs. Therefore, I was the perfect candidate to be bullied.

I was called a werewolf and witch by the "old kids." They seemed to have the law on their side because their parents were the Khmer Rouge supporters. I chose to remain quiet. I did my work each day to earn my daily ratio of food to eat. I stayed mostly by myself because we were not encouraged to make friends. Somehow, the revolution instilled fear in all of us. We were not to trust anyone. Mom told me not to trust anyone, either.

Twice a week, we were allowed to go to the lake to clean ourselves. I used to bathe in the water with my clothes on, scrubbing myself as best as I could. There was no shampoo or soap, so I used my hands to brush the dirt off my shirt and pants. Being allowed to wash in the nearby lake felt like a luxury. I did not care what was in the water; I stayed as long as I could in the lake. I mostly soaked myself in the shallow end. I did not know how to swim. I would never go to the deep end.

There was a day when I stood in the sun to dry myself with my clothes on. I felt itchy between my legs. I scratched myself. Suddenly, this awful creature fell off. It was a leech. It was about six or seven inches long. When it fell to the ground, it curled up from one end to another to protect the blood that was distorted in my body. I did not know how long it had sucked my blood. It had been there long enough to fall on its own when it filled its body with blood. I watched others trying to pull leeches away from their bodies before. It was not simple. Leeches had mouths on both ends. When it grabbed onto your skin, it hung on tightly on both ends. I was shivering as I looked at my leech on the ground. I left it there to find its own way to live.

Walking by the riverbank before returning to camp, I sensed a few older kids watching me.

Suddenly, one of the kids approached me quickly, and I was unprepared to be sent down to the river below. There were bushes and rocks on the way down to the water. The girl was bigger than me. She had more power. I felt like I was flying in that second, except I bumped into some rock or some kind of bushes. There was no one there to help me. I felt myself drinking some water, but I was not sinking. In fact, I remembered choking and floating at the same time. It was weird. It was like I had helium inside me. Somehow, I was pushing myself to shore. Once I had my foot stable on the ground, I coughed hard a few times. I was lightheaded.

There was the current, but I was not swept away with it. I was able to crawl up to the riverbank slowly.

My face was hurting. I coughed until all the water seemed to be gone. Every time I spit out the water, I saw blood. I knew that I hit my face as I plunged down. I had no mirror. I did not see what I looked like.

I felt a bit dizzy. I was not sure where I got hit on the way down. Was it my head? Suddenly, I felt a sharp pain in my face and in my mouth. I used my hand to feel my own face. I did not seem to have any gash on my face. I used my index finger to feel my mouth. I found the source of the pain. The inside skin of my mouth was cut. It was the cause of the bleeding. I also discovered that the two fangs were broken off. It explained the bleeding pain in my mouth.

Somehow, I managed to walk back to the sleeping area. Without reporting the incident, I cried to myself to sleep. I slept through the night without eating until daylight. If someone were to see what had happened to me, that individual would not say anything anyway.

After all, we were taught to look out for just ourselves.

Klune Thee Penk Klune (self-depends on self).

A revolution that intended to level the playing field by eliminating competition, classes, wealth, and status gave contradictory messages. If I could only depend on myself to survive, why would it prevent me from being self-sufficient? Perhaps it meant that when it came to hostility, no one was willing to put themselves at risk to help others. I had no one to rely on. I had no hope of being reunited with Mom again. I was just waiting around for my turn to end that suffering.

It had been weeks since I was pushed off the cliff into the lake. The benefit of being young was that the body healed quickly without penicillin.

I continued to keep to myself. I worked all day plowing the field. By this time, the only clothing I had on began to depreciate. It was easily ripped. The long pants became shorter. The living conditions were terrible, and it was not a place where people could stay healthy for long. The camp was only meant to be a temporary shelter. There was nothing about it that could support a child's growth or stable future. It was not a surprise. Since we were placed there as laborers. Ultimately, the Khmer Rouge aimed to destroy all city dwellers, including children.

As I recall, there were more children at the camp than when I first arrived. Within months, I noticed there was less. I kept to myself every day. I talked to no one. No one talked to me. We were not supposed to socialize. Perhaps this was the strategy of the Khmer Rouge all along. No one would miss anyone because there was no connection between them. The children lacked a support system. We were discouraged from helping each other. It was about self-preservation. It was "Klune Thee Penk Klune." "ខ្លួនទីពឹងខ្លួន."

On the other hand, I saw nothing because I protected my own sanity. I could only take so much. Watching my three brothers die one by one in the most horrific ways to die was enough for me. Therefore, to keep on living, I adopted the term "see no evil, hear no evil."

As weeks went by, I was not sure if the work became harder or if my body began to degrade due to insufficient nutrients. I could hardly lift a hoe above my head. The soil was dry and made it harder for me to plow. I began to panic. Then, I wished for the rain. It would help to soften the soil for me to spend less energy to get the task done. I was genuinely worried about the consequences of not completing my task for the first time. My thoughts went wild. It was the concept of Angka of "no benefit to keep me" when I became unproductive. Then, I thought about what Mom said: that my father and brothers were now free from life's suffering. I, too, wanted to be free from life's suffering. However, I did not want the slow agony of dying the way my brothers did. If I could just lie down and sleep forever, I would be satisfied.

Thinking about how my brothers died still broke my heart. I could never understand why anyone would be so cruel to children, no matter the reason. I blamed the adults for this act of revenge. The teachings about respecting elders were no longer relevant. I felt betrayed by the teaching of "no harm" to others. At this point, I was still a kid. I was helpless in the circumstances that I was in. I had to play it by ear to see what came next since I had no control over my surroundings. Suddenly, I heard someone approach me.

"Hey, kid." She called out.

"I'll help you with your row." She took the hoe from my hands and began to plow for me. I was confused.

Suddenly, someone helped me. She was not afraid to be punished by the group leader. Apparently, she had some privileges in the camp. I believe we crossed paths at the previous camp. She was certainly older than me and much bigger in physical appearance. She could plow quickly. She did not seem to suffer from malnutrition like I was. Suddenly, I felt like I had my own fairy godmother. I was overwhelmed and puzzled by the kind gestures.

"Call me Mett Srey." She introduced herself. It was like she approached me with a mission. I was sure there were weaker kids than I was. She seemed to come to my aid at the crucial moment.

I did not deny the assistance. She seemed to have access to local resources. I was no longer being bullied. The kids who wanted to punish me stayed far away because of Srey. I was baffled by Srey's sudden help but didn't seek an explanation. I was afraid of losing support. Nevertheless,

Srey restored some of my belief in human kindness when I thought the concept of "kindness and compassion" as part of a good human being was all a lie and did not exist. Srey showed me that it still does.

At nighttime, Srey would sneak extra sweet rice or sweet potato for me. She was careful not to let others see us. However, she was among the "old kids." Because of her status, she had more privileges, and no one questioned why she was helping me. For the first time in a long while, I felt a sense of relief. Since Baron's death, I never thought I would survive this long. The harsh reality had become too much to bear. Receiving help from someone on the other side was unexpected, but it gave me hope and the courage to stop fearing the consequences. Since the beginning of the Khmer Rouge, I had no friends. I had my brothers. We were between the ages of five to nine at the time. When we got so hungry, we used to reminisce about the good old days when we had so much to eat. We swore with each other that if we lived to see those foods again, we would never take anything for granted. When all my brothers died, I became deaf, blind, dumb, and filled with ignorance. I had to be able to keep on breathing.

For the first time, someone was there to help me. I had someone to talk to. I was uncertain if it was a trick or genuine, but I no longer concerned myself with the future. I just decided to go with the flow. In that moment, I actually felt happy. I remembered what Mom said, "trust no one." At this point, I had no other good option. If my time came to join my brothers and father, I would not regret making friends before the end of my life.

Every evening, Srey would come to sit with me through the darkness of night. I found out that she could not read or write. She was older than me. She could have if there were opportunities for her.

"Do you know of any bedtime stories?" I asked.

"No," she said with curiosity. Stories allowed imagination. Stories trigger the conscience of individuals to think about what is right and wrong. To limit children with hope and imagination is destroying the future of any nation. How was it possible that I was able to learn, and she was not? I was not proud that I knew how to read, even though not fluently, but I had access to education.

She did not have the same view of the importance of having the ability to read and write. It seemed to me that life for her was all about sustaining the daily routine. There was no question of what could have been if one were to be educated. She accepted her life as if it was just the way things were meant to be. This differed greatly from my family's experience. Mom and Dad treated each other as equals, sharing both respect and responsibility. They wanted to change the old ways from Mak Yay's generation, where women weren't allowed to get an education. If Mak Yay was not determined to change her faith, she would be in the same boat as Srey's parents. They accepted life as it was. Yet they were told to persecute those who somehow did them wrong, the city dwellers. Srey did not seem to regret not knowing how to read and write.

"You know bedtime stories?" she asked me reluctantly.

"Yes, I remember some." I was no longer afraid of revealing my identity to a child who was born in the city and was allowed to go to school. I remembered many bedtime stories. Mom or Yay Reun sometimes shared it. The scary story that I remember was "Neang 12 Nak" (12 Ladies). It was supposed to be related to the history of how angels (Tevada) changed the course of hate to love and justice. However, the traumatic portion was overwhelming for my young age. There were other stories that I enjoyed. One of my favorites was The Rabbit and the Snail. It was the version of Tortoise and the Hare.

In Cambodian culture and throughout history, rabbits are considered intelligent and sophisticated. More importantly, rabbits were considered honorable and crafty. Whoever is born under the animal sign of the rabbit in the lunar year is considered intelligent.

To pass the time, I tried to remember the bedtime story I was told before the Khmer Rouge took over. In my mind, I retold it as best as I could. A long time ago, a rabbit was hopping along when it came across a beautiful pond filled with green lotus leaves and water lilies. The rabbit was enchanted and thirsty. Immediately, it drank the water. Suddenly, the rabbit heard a noise.

"Disrespectful," a voice was a bit louder.

"Who's there?" asked the rabbit, trying hard to look for the owner of the sound.

"Here I am," said the snail, showing his proud and small features.

"Why did you say that I was being disrespectful?" asked the rabbit.

"Because you drank water from this pond without asking for permission," said the snail.

"Someone owns this pond?" the rabbit asked sarcastically. The pond was in the wild. It was left for wild animals to enjoy. Why did I have to ask permission to enjoy the cold water from the aroma of nature and flowers? I enjoyed my day running through the beautiful wilderness. There was no one for me to ask permission from, thought the rabbit. How ridiculous it was for the snail to suggest that the pond had an owner?

"I live in this pond. Therefore, it is mine." Said the Snail.

"Then, what can I do to drink more of the water?" Rabbit asked politely.

"How's about a race?" Said the snail.

"A race?" The rabbit was puzzled yet thought about the unfair competition between the rabbit and the snail. The rabbit thought of how dare the snail consider himself equal to the four-legged and beautiful fur with quick thinking. The rabbit thought there was no match. The snail couldn't win.

"What is the condition?" asked the rabbit.

"If you win, you can drink the pond water whenever you like without asking for permission." Snail explained. "If you lose, you can never drink the pond water."

"Deal." The rabbit eagerly agreed. It was a race around the pond. How could I lose with the fastest speed that I practiced every day?

The snail, however, knew that it was not the strength that could win the bet. It was all about planning.

"Ready. Set," said the snail. The rabbit ran confidently, thinking that he would always be ahead of the snail no matter what. As he ran, he called out to the snail to check its position. But each time, the snail somehow answered from ahead of him. The rabbit was confused. How could the snail be in front? The rabbit forced himself to run even faster. Whenever the rabbit asked, "Where are you?" it seemed like the snail was already ahead in the front. Exhausted, as the rabbit made the round of the pond, it stopped.

The snail was already at the finish line. Embarrassed, the rabbit apologized for being arrogant, thinking that the race was too easy, and promised never to drink the pond water ever again. It was said that the wild rabbit only drank water from grasses or leaves for moisture but never pond water, as the saying goes.

However, the moral of the story was about respect and consideration. I am reminded of traditional and religious beliefs. It is our tradition or superstition whenever we settled in a new place, whether a country, home, apartment, or outdoors, I quietly seek permission to stay by praying to the invisible protector of the land or space before us. Mak Yay or Mom would light three incenses as they prayed for safety. It is a great practice to be considerate and kind, not only to others but to unforeseen forces as well. For example, when I moved to a new home, Mom requested that the Buddhist monk does the blessing for us, where the monks chanted the verse and scattered holy water for "Trojak Trojom" (meaning warmth, spirit, and peace). The assumption is that each space has its own protector. The Buddhist ritual is the formal asking for peace and safety.

Many nights, I shared folk tales with Srey to pass the time. Sometimes, when I was exhausted from the hard labor, I slept soundly, allowing the time to pass by. Yet, there were many nights when I was not sure of what the future would be like for me. I was in a child labor camp. There was no escape but fear for the time to vanish into thin air. When children died, there was no one to mourn their deaths. The body was taken away into the night. There was no funeral. There was no Buddhist monk blessing. How long would Mom know about my death when it was my turn? I heard that my father died for at least six months before the news was shared with Mom. I assumed the same thing when it came to me.

However, one night, Srey whispered to me.

"I'm going to take you out of this camp?" She was so confident about her decision.

"Huh!" I was dumbfounded.

"We will escape from the camp." She continued. I was still confused. More importantly, I was not sure whether I should trust her or continue to survive the uncertainty of being confined to a controlled environment. I saw many examples of kids trying to escape the camp. I would not dare to risk my life. However, what kind of life would I have waiting for my turn? I was safe so far because I followed the rules. What happens when I break the rules?

"We're going to my village." Srey insisted. I guessed the thought of reuniting with Mom was enough for me to consider the risk factors. Srey belonged to the "old people" group. She would not face severe punishment if she got caught. After all, she belonged to the protected class.

But if I got caught, I would be sentenced to death for trying to escape. The camp was a place where city children were forced to work without enough food, medical care, or anyone to look after them until they died. What kind of government would do such a thing to children? Sometimes, I thought that my brothers were lucky to die early without facing such physical, emotional, and mental abuse as me.

Thus far, Srey has helped me to survive. I should take the risk with her. I had nothing to lose. If I stayed any longer in the camp, I might face other dangers. The thought of reuniting with Mom kept giving me hope.

"My mother will help you to find your mother," she explained further.

It seemed like Srey's mother knew my mother. I had to put my faith in Srey. Angka's word of

"ខ្លួនទីពឹងខ្លួន" (Self depends on self) might not apply to me

in this sense. I needed to trust Srey completely. I was not familiar with my surroundings. I did not even know what province I was in. Growing up in the city, I had not seen this much of the inhabited areas. I would be lost in the wild if, somehow, I was lost in the jungle. Besides, I would not know where to go if I was free. It was like I had been blindfolded for years. I was immune to following directions, and I could not navigate myself out of a dangerous camp.

There was no better option for me. I had to be courageous. I needed to be brave like my brother Baron if I wanted to see Mom again. The thought of Baron gave me the confidence to say "yes." Srey was happy with my decision. She did not have to convince me any further. At this point, I had no control over what would happen. I just needed to follow Srey's instructions on what came next.

Srey told me to be prepared. In two days, we will leave the camp. I was not sure how she selected the day to leave. Srey was a few years older than I was. Maybe she knew how the camp worked. She definitely had more access than I did. She told me we had to leave early, preferably before dawn, when everyone was still asleep. Srey instructed me to meet her behind the banana trees near the communal kitchen. Since it was still dark before dawn, the morning fog would help hide us from the view. Srey told me that the journey on foot to her village would take the entire day. I had no idea what kind of route we would take to prevent us from being caught. The anticipation of the journey left me restless. However, Srey was calm and always snuck extra food for me to eat. When the day came, I would have the energy to walk. The day did come. My heart was beating faster than I could count. I wondered if Mom knew what I was about to do. She would never approve of escaping from the camp that I was required to be in. This children's camp was the toughest for me because no adults seemed to care about the future of the children. It was like a survival game where the toughest one lived, and the weaker one died.

Srey met me at the rendezvous place before dawn.

"Let's go." She whispered.

I took a deep breath and began to follow each step behind her. I walked through the jungle quietly, afraid to look around in case I saw anything else within my view. We followed only a small trail, and sometimes, I did not see the walking trail. Srey took me on the trail. Perhaps it was a shortcut to her village.

I saw nothing but wild nature. The thick green forest seemed to be watching me. I was afraid to even look up to appreciate the tall trees that had been there for centuries. I had no clue of the names for each tree. I only knew how uncertain the condition of my environment.

Srey seemed to know her way around the forest. We walked without stopping. Suddenly, the sun began to show how bright and how hot it could warm Mother Earth. It had been hours already since we walked. I had no idea how far or where we were. My pace began to slow down. Suddenly, I stumbled and fell to the ground. I sat still as though my feet refused to take any more steps. I had been abusing my feet long enough. I walked with no shoes for miles in the jungle.

"What?" Srey asked, disappointed that I stopped.

"We have to make it to my village before nightfall," she demanded.

"My feet," I mumbled, pointing to the cracks and blisters at the bottoms of my feet.

Srey had a rubber sandal like many "old people" did. She realized that I had no shoes on. One great thing about Cambodia's nature, there are always banana trees nearby. Quickly, Srey cut out a banana tree. She peeled off each layer to find a perfect one for me. She helped me clean out the splinters before wrapping the cool layer from the banana tree onto my feet. She used the dead outer layer as a final string to hold it together as though she were making temporary shoes for me to walk in.

She was resourceful. I was amazed at how attentive she was to me. We continued walking along the path that she had made for me. Because as children, we were told that mines could be everywhere if we defied Angka's wishes and attempted to escape. I was able to continue walking without feeling the pain as much.

The sun was about to set when we reached a village. It looked familiar, but I did not know when we settled there. Srey handed me off to her mother and left. I was given food. I was told to hide between the vegetable barrels and other supplies. The produce would be sent to Mom's camp. The ox cart driver asked me to stay still until I got there. I slept, putting my head on both knees, sitting straight up, and hugging my knees for support. I had to sit like that for hours to come.

It was from dawn to almost sunset. When the man stopped to unload at the community kitchen when he told me to get off, and it took me a while to stand up because I was in the same position for so long.

The man pointed me in the direction of multiple huts lined up, where I saw many women wearing black almost looked like a special force. They were the team of great producers for Angka.

I walked without certainty of what was going to happen to me; then I saw Mom. It was a moment of truth.

Reunited With Mom

Mom was overjoyed when she saw me, tears of relief washing down her face. She believed that Buddha answered her prayer. She did good deeds in her life. It was the least compensation that she would get was to reunite with me. Not knowing how I was doing for months, even years, it took a toll on her mental health. She was over the moon even though our condition was not improving. We still lived under the watchful eyes of Angka, who decided our fate at any moment.

On the other hand, I attributed my good fortune to Srey, who cleverly navigated the direction out of the children's camp. The camp was about to be abandoned again, and weaker children were somehow disappearing into the night. There was no way of knowing my turn if Srey was not there to aid in my hardship.

Apparently, I found out that Srey was Mitt Nang's daughter. Mitt Nang was once Mom section leader. She was among the "old people." She had more privilege than us. Obviously, Mitt Nang used her daughter to get me out of the children's camp. Mom confessed that she often pleaded with Mitt Nang every time she saw her to help get me out. Eventually, Mitt Nang changed her mind. She decided to help Mom after seeing how hard she worked every day. Mom was as skilled as those who had grown up planting rice their whole lives. Even after losing her husband and three sons, she put all her energy into her work. She was soon moved up the rank to the most "productive unit" with a bit more food. Perhaps Mitt Nang suddenly realized how incredible Mom was. Mitt Nang compelled me to ensure that Mom would get me in return. The intention to penalize all city dwellers had become questionable in section leaders such as Mitt Nang.

Perhaps the fact that Mom did not break after the death of her three sons and husband gave a strong impression on Mett Nang. Or perhaps Mitt Nang tried to redeem herself in the eyes of Buddha. Nevertheless, there was compassion after all. Even among the Khmer Rouge supporters, there would be one person who could change the outcome of the other. It was Mett Nang who cared about Mom after watching her heartbroken each time her loved one died.

Anyhow, as I reunited with Mom, she requested permission to keep me by her side. Once again, I had to work as an adult to earn a daily ratio of food. By this time, the search for supplements was less strict. Mom and I were able to add vegetables to the rice portion we gathered in the field. The extra protein I ate came from different kinds of snails. There were land snails, which were bigger, and I found them by digging or plowing the field. There were also freshwater snails, which were smaller but plentiful. I could scoop up several at once. Mom would cut a piece of cloth and sew it inside my shirt where I could store what I found in the field to take back to our shed. The lucrative commodities during the Khmer Rouge were salt and sugar. Mom would trade any value she had left for just a teaspoon of salt.

Mom and I were happy that we got to work together. We shared the same shed. We were more creative with our minimum nutrition. We did not get sick. We were productive citizens of the Khmer Rouge.

After a long day of work and giving our bodies enough nutrition to keep us moving, we slept like babies. Mom had a bamboo mattress that was above the ground. I was steady for both of us. Perhaps I did not notice anything uncomfortable because I was tired most nights. Once my body lay straight, I was out.

One night, I was startled by the shadow of a man coming into our shed. I could feel the wind blowing as our mosquito net was opened. Suddenly, I felt Mom push me to the side, shielding me with her body. I could smell the scent of a man. There was definitely someone who had entered our sleeping space that night. Maybe it was just a bad dream. I wished it were. Somehow, I fell back asleep. When I woke up at dawn, Mom was already awake. She did not say anything. She reported to work early as usual. I reported to work as well. I was tired from physical labor. I did not have the energy to recall what I saw as a shadow or just fear.

Working in the Cambodian community decades later, I heard many survivors, especially women, share their trauma of having a physical assault by the Khmer Rouge men. Why is it that when there is war, there is hatred toward women? Or is it an opportunity for men to force themselves on women?

It was not until I heard many women admit that they faced sexual assaults during the Khmer Rouge. Somehow, when there were war or domestic issues, women were always at the mercy of the perpetrators. The Cambodian culture also taught women to be reserved and submissive. It allowed men without conscience to act on their impulse, knowing that women would not speak of the violation because the culture deemed to blame women. No one dared to admit to the assault on their bodies without their approval.

In many ways, I was proud of the women who attended the Cambodian community center and shared their stories with me. I heard about the intentional separation when the Khmer Rouge leader saw beautiful city women with husbands and children; they would separate the husbands, then the children, so that the women would become their prey. Young women were also a target.

I was glad that I was young enough not to have to go through what they went through. I was twelve in the last year of the Khmer Rouge. Mom never confirmed what had happened that night. I did not want to trigger any trauma for her. Therefore, I considered these memories as nightmares. Still, I was angry to know that when there is war, women are always the victims of vicious violations of their dignity. Why must men rob women of their self-worth with their invasion of the private space? How can I ever see the good in humans after knowing such an event happened again and again when it came to war?

It was almost the end of the Khmer Rouge. Yet, the camp that Mom and I were in was still in isolation. We were still held captive by the Khmer Rouge to work. There was nowhere in sight of a civilization. I had not seen a bed with a soft mattress for almost four years. I had not felt the warm water running out from a faucet for so long. I began to feel comfortable walking at the campground with security guards hidden to see if I would violate any rules in order to punish me. I would not know where to go outside of the parameters of the camp.

That evening, I wandered around the edge of the camp to stretch my legs. Our shed was so small that there was only enough space to sleep, there was no room to walk. I was not sure why I decided to go outside. Mom usually warned me to stay out of sight because most people in her camp were adults. But since it was still lighting out, I decided to walk around. The evening air gave me a bit of a chill, considering that I had recovered from malaria. However, being near Mom, she patched up my shirt with different materials that she was able to find. Perhaps some of them came from the people who had already died. I needed to have at least full coverage of a shirt than what I had during the children's camp.

For a moment, I actually enjoyed the rusty campground surrounded by nature. I thought I was free to roam around the camp.

As I was lost in my own thoughts, there were flying objects dropping down from the sky. They were papers. I had not seen papers in years. One sheet landed right in front of me. I was curious, however hesitant, about what to do. Should I pick it up or walk past it? I stood still for a while, deciding what to do. Wasn't I supposed to be illiterate?

Without further hesitation, I picked it up. I began to read what was written on the paper. Before I could make out the rest of the words, Mom snatched it away from me. I had no idea where she came from. She was faster than lightning. Her eyes glared at me as though she had been possessed by evil. I was not sure whether she was angry or horrified.

"What are you doing with that?" she scolded.

"Don't pretend that you can read, stupid child," she yelled loud enough that people could hear her. She threw the paperback on the ground as though she did not care about it. She took my hand and walked back to our shed as though to give me further discipline.

I was still in shock at her reaction. However, further away from us, I did notice the Khmer Rouge soldiers with guns watching and observing our behaviors. They were the guards, making sure that we could not escape the camp.

When we got back to our shed, Mom checked to see if we had not been followed. Finally, we were all alone, quietly, Mom asked.

"What did it say?"

"Something about help on the way?" I did not finish reading. I was not supposed to read, yet I was surprised that I still could. Mom warned me about doing things out in the open. The eyes were watching.

I realized that I put a target on our backs. The Khmer Rouge attempted to eliminate all with the ability to read and write. Mom and I would be discovered. No matter how much Mom tried to convince them that we were just a working-class family from the city, we were not ordinary. We had survived this long. Mom was inspired by what she heard. We did not know who was sending the messages, but whoever it was, they gave us hope. We had to stay alive no matter what. Mom quietly gathered information. She noticed the panic among the Khmer Rouge leaders. She told me to be strong and brave. Whatever came next for us, we had to persevere some more. Mom faced many crisis moments during the Khmer Rouge, but dying was not an option. She could not bear having me belong to the Khmer Rouge. My mother possessed a commendable ability to maintain hope.

A few weeks later, Mom was told we were being relocated. It was toward the end of the harvest season. Meaning we are now in the spring season. It was the spring of 1979. Somehow, we were pushed deeper into the rural area where people were sent for reeducation. Meaning there was no future or hope for those who were sent to do the canal work.

Mom was not comfortable with the word "relocation." She knew what it meant for us. We were now expendable. Our names were on the relocation list.

She did not tell me in detail what would happen. But I was quick to see her expression of hopelessness. No one would help us now. Our time had come to say goodbye to this cruelest world. Mom did her best to protect me. It was now up to faith to determine whether we should live or die.

I could not help but wonder if it was my fault. Was it because of the paper that I picked up and read? Mom never explained why. It was beyond our control.

As we assembled for further instruction, names were called to be shipped out. There were at least twenty-five of us. We were to march in a straight line. There were the Khmer Rouge soldiers on horses with guns.

At that moment, Mom knew that our journey would end that day. She did not tell me that our relocation was the last trip that we would ever walk on for the rest of our lives. I knew as much as I looked at the expression of sadness all around me. There was no explanation from Angka for our crimes. We faced execution.

Without saying a word to me, she grabbed my hand to walk side by side within one line. I saw a couple of other kids. But I was completely focused on Mom. It had been a long-lasting suffering. I would welcome the opportunity to be free from life-suffering, according to Buddha and Mom.

I do not remember how we got there, but I clearly remember standing by the canal that Mom had helped dig, waiting to be executed. Looking back, it felt strange. Why did we just stand there, helpless, when there were so many of us and only a few men on horseback? A woman standing to the right side of Mom was crying hysterically. Suddenly, she stopped crying. She looked angry as she stared at Mom.

Was she angry at us for showing no emotion? Did she think that we were not normal in terms of showing no fear? She could not take the silence from Mom and me. Did she not know that Mom and I saw death more often than we wished not to see? She was infuriated at us for seeming not to grasp the situation we found ourselves in.

"You and your daughter are about to be killed," she uttered, almost shouting to get Mom's attention. She seemed angry at us.

"How was it that you were not crying?" The woman seemed to be mad at us rather than to be afraid of what came next. The woman did not know that Mom had already lost her husband and three sons. What else could she do as she and I were about to be put down permanently?

Sure, it did not look like we were afraid because we were already tired of living in this horrible world, seeing mankind as evil. If we wanted to cry, there would be no more tears. I did not understand why we were jealous; we just did not panic. Regardless, I heard nothing from Mom except the words, "At least we will all be together," Mom said casually. It was like she had no more energy to argue with fate. I agreed with her. I just wanted to be with my family again. I longed for the afterlife, where I could see my three brothers and father. Mom found comfort in her belief in Buddha, where death meant the end of life's suffering. It was probably the end of feeling hungry and wishing that I could go back to the time when food was not such a valuable commodity. I felt relieved to see the afterlife, knowing I would avoid witnessing older people treating younger ones as worthless and less human.

Mom was immobile. Yet, she tightened her grip as she held my hand. I could hear her heartbeat faster. From the outside, she appeared to be calm, but on the inside, she was frightened. I was uncertain whether her concern was for my well-being or her own. Even in death she wanted to die with dignity. She refused to express her anger and hatred of the revolution which intent to rid certain groups of people. She was not going to cry, beg, or whine. Mom knew how to shield her fear very well. Perhaps, if she showed any weakness, her perpetrators would win. Or perhaps, she would shatter into pieces of all the things that she witnessed and took away from her.

There was nothing for me to focus on while waiting to be killed. My eyes wandered all over the place. When I looked down at my feet, I realized that I had no shoes. I began to regret dying without wearing shoes. Suddenly, I wondered what if I could not run or walk as fast in my afterlife when I would leave this world without shoes. I envisioned a peaceful afterlife where I started over as a child, free from hunger. I even smiled at the thought of reuniting with my brothers. At the same time, I thought of the unjust and cruel environment I had faced as a child.

Mom and I stood next to each other with our own thoughts when all I heard was "move" or "run." I did not know which one.

I only remember running away from the Khmer Rouge soldiers. It felt like my longest run ever.

Mom said that I was so sick afterward. She thought that I was not about to make it. I did not remember being ill, but I remembered being chased. Mom and I camped on the ground in the wild, trying to find our way out of the jungle.

Mom knew that the country was in chaos once more. This time, it was Vietnam that invaded Cambodia. Rumors that the Vietnamese government would kill Khmer citizens were spreading. Mom was not sure where to go. We ran with a small group of people in fear. We wanted to find some type of civilization. We had been too deep into the jungle.

I remembered we crossed a lake. Some people used all kinds of dry logs to get themselves across to the other side. Some adults swam. I was no more than four feet at that time. I did not know how to swim. Mom did not know how to swim either. Yet, she pulled me along as we crossed the lake without knowing how deep it was. I remembered she grabbed me by the hair following other people as the Khmer Rouge soldiers chased us. Mom did not even think about drowning. Her mission was not to get both of us killed. I felt submerged at first. However, mom held onto my hair. I was able to come up for air one in a while. Somehow, I was floating alongside Mom. Miraculously, we made it to the other side of the lake. It was the most memorable moment of my life. I had no idea how Mom did it. She was fearless. It was running toward civilization. It was like she knew that she would not allow the end of us to go down easily. I was able to walk on a concrete street once more.

Chapter Four
Post Khmer Rouge

Uncertainty

After Vietnam ousted the Khmer Rouge in late 1978, my mother and I made our ways in the rubble of the cities by in 1979. Having been trapped in the jungle and pursued by Khmer Rouge soldiers, we were wary of returning home, especially given the uncertainty and the presence of Vietnamese forces on major roads. Instead, my mother chose to relocate to Battambang province. Without relatives or connections there, we spent some time searching for acquaintances. In retrospect, I understand her reluctance to return home immediately; having lost her husband and three sons, she likely found it too painful to face the past. Relocating allowed us to avoid immediate reminders of our loss and provided the freedom to move forward.

Even though Vietnam disposed of the Khmer Rouge, people were more afraid of the Vietnamese than the Khmer Rouge. I was a bit confused by the adult's perception until I learned that Mom's generation inherited hatred toward Vietnam and its people because of their goals. To put it simply, Vickery (1984) confirmed that there was no surprise that the Vietnamese government intended to absorb Cambodia and make into an annex of Vietnam, where the Khmer people would become second-class citizens. Because of this known objective, the Khmer people were willing to trust others, except the Vietnamese. They also forgot that there were ordinary Vietnamese people that the French brought in to work under their colonial administration, who had mixed families in Cambodia as well. Despite tensions between the Khmer Rouge and the Vietnamese Cambodian, there were exchanges of rice seeds for weapons with North

Vietnam. It was all about politics. Nevertheless, individuals experienced loss and hardship due to the animosity and avarice exhibited by neighboring countries.

Mom was also concerned about the Vietnamese's. She was taught to be suspicious of their intention.

Anyhow, she wanted to go to Battambang to find her friend, Ming Vee. It was Ming Vee's hometown. She was also Mom's neighbor in Phnom Penh. She lost her husband and two children; one was a baby, and the other was a toddler. She had no one to go back to Phnom Penh. Perhaps Mom felt the same way.

When we first reunited with Ming Vee, we sat for hours in silence. I knew that she and her Mom tried to process the pains of losing a husband and children. If there were tears, I would expect they were completely dehydrated from walking and trying to find the direction of where, what, and how to move on after the three years and eight months of such atrocity.

Then, suddenly, my stomach gave a signal of life. My body was still functioning. I needed fuel to continue. Ming Vee found one small yam for me. It was the best that I ever ate. It was free, and it was given to me. I did not have to earn it by digging dirt or carrying hay. Mom and Ming Vee realized that there was more to life than just resigning to the pain of losses. I was there. What would become of me if my mother decided to end her life after enduring such immense hardship? After all, Mom still needed to find closure. She was searching for family members.

Ming Vee and Mom registered with the local authority and began to find work, hoping to meet someone who might encounter the family.

I did not know how to keep track of the time we spent in Battambang province. It was Mom who was the wanderer.

We had no home and no one to go back to Phnom Penh. Maybe she felt a bit better being around a friend and neighbor who, like her, had lost everything. Meanwhile, I got used to farm life with Ming Vee's family. I helped grow corn, tomatoes, potatoes, and many types of green vegetables. We had plenty of food to eat. We traded our vegetables for things we didn't have, like salt and sugar. Our living conditions were not well in terms of clothing and hygiene products. Mom noticed that she and I had lice. So, she shaved both of our hair off. During the Khmer Rouge, we were not allowed to keep our hair past our shoulders anyway. They would just cut it off about the neck without trimming.

I wondered how I looked back then. There was no photo to show me how I looked during the Khmer Rouge. Even after the Khmer Rouge, I never encountered a mirror or even had the need to want to know how I looked. After Mom shaved my head, I heard some adults tell me that I looked like a boy. I knew that I was skinny when I was encouraged to eat more.

In my memories, I only saw the images of my father and brothers when they died. The word inhumane would not be enough to describe how they looked to me.

At any rate, Mom and I met the bare minimum of our physiological needs. However, according to Maslow's hierarchy of needs, the next step of needs would be safety. It was clear that we did not achieve safety. Mom and I doubted the current administration under the Vietnamese leadership of the country. Every time I saw a Vietnamese soldier with a gun on the street; my heartbeat grew faster. Mom remained vigilant and under the radar as though an unknown group was secretly hunting us down.

In the meantime, there was no schooling for me. I had no schooling during the Khmer Rouge except the teaching of propaganda on how to contribute to the State; otherwise, one would not be worthy of being alive.

I was only looking for food. I had no vision of schooling. There was none anyway during the transition and the aftermath of such an atrocity.

Mom focused all her energy on finding her siblings. I was left to do what I could to gather food. We slept on the floor for months. Yet, we had no complaints. Perhaps, we were not under the watchful eyes of Angka. When Mom got news of her surviving siblings, we vacated our temporary housing at once. We journeyed back to Phnom Penh for the first time after the Khmer Rouge. Mom had no plan to introduce me to the home that I had lost, but only to find her family. It was all about who was living and who was dead.

Mom's four younger siblings were all alive. They were teenagers, and one was a young adult when the Khmer Rouge took over. All of them had gone to school in Phnom Penh. The sister, who was the oldest, was in medical school at the time. Mom worried about their survivor rate being college students. They were evacuated to the countryside, where their uncle helped protect their identities and ensured their safety. However, Mom gets the news that her father is not so lucky. He and his second wife, plus three children, did not make it. Grandfather Sok's health was degrading day by day until he passed. As for mom's stepmother and three half-siblings, they were killed.

Mom was eager to see her siblings, so we left Battambang quickly. We did not own anything, so we traveled with just what we had on. I remembered riding on a freight train to Phnom Penh.

First, we met Mom's brother, Serei, who was nineteen when the Khmer Rouge took over. Serei meant Free in English. Now, he was twenty-four with an eight-month-old daughter and a wife. She was the nuptial that the Khmer

Rouge forced him to consummate. He brought her to the city, where he worked in transportation. He knew how to drive, so he drove a big truck, moving unknown supplies for government contractors. The country was in a transition to a new government under the control of Vietnam. He worked for food, supplies, and apartments. Wages were not established then.

He allowed Mom and I to stay in his apartment while we were back in Phnom Penh.

Mom did not dare to go anywhere near our home. She did not want to remember her losses. I guessed it was too difficult for her to see a place where she shared great memories with her dad and all her children. If she saw an empty place with broken glass and trash everywhere, as we saw in the city when we came to the street where Uncle Serei lived, we would feel the sense of emptiness and the hollow in our hearts. The only mission Mom had in coming to Phnom Penh was to convince her surviving siblings to leave the country with her and me.

It appears Mom was afraid of the "historic enemy"-the Vietnamese. Now that Vietnam had control of Cambodia, she had no hope. When the Khmer Rouge soldiers were chasing us, they did say that the "Vietnamese will have no mercy on you." I understood why Mom wanted to leave Cambodia as soon as possible.

In the meantime, the living conditions of Uncle Serei's apartment were deplorable. We could smell human waste everywhere. We met Uncle Serei's wife and child. They stayed on the cleaner side of the same apartment as though the smell did not bother them. The toddler was a girl. She would crawl all over the place.

Mom asked why the toddler wouldn't wear any clothes. His wife answered, "It would soon be dirty again." The justification was that I saw naked children running around in the countryside with no clothes on because it was easier to clean. It would be in the dirt and become natural fertilizer anyway. Mom realized her brother needed help adjusting to city life with his wife, who was from a rural area, as the Khmer Rouge intended when they forced him to marry at the end of the revolution. The result of that action against his will was the daughter. He did not have the heart to abandon her like his brother did.

Mom sympathized with her brother and tried as much as she could to support the living conditions. She had me down on my knees, sweeping the tile floor. I was happy to sleep on the tile for the first time after the Khmer Rouge. I was surprised that I did not miss what bed felt like when I slept. I remember I used to sleep in bed.

Anyhow, I wonder what the purpose of forced marriage during the Khmer Rouge regime was. Was it just about procreation, as they claimed? Or was it more sinister than that? Was it to experience the co-existence between different backgrounds of individuals? I thought the Khmer Rouge despised city dwellers, thinking that all city dwellers were corrupt, including children. Then, why would they arrange for city-born young men to marry countryside young women? What was the purpose of procreating mixed backgrounds? Was it to use some knowledge between those who were exposed to education and foreign influence on young women who had never known the outside world, let alone be literate in their own language? Uncle Serei was wild and free. To stay alive, he submitted to the Khmer Rouge's forced marriage. However, he put less effort into ensuring mutual respect and love after he made a family. He was angry about what he had to endure, yet he held on to the family without his consent.

I wondered why Uncle Serei did not just leave her and the daughter to start fresh after the revolution. Knowing him, he was tough on the outside but soft on the inside. He could never abandon his child, whether it was by force of choice. He felt obligated to take care of the kid and the wife. He brought his wife and daughter to America. He was hoping to start a new life, free from trauma, as he embraced the unity of his mother and siblings. However, he was unaware that life in the city was different because he had come from a city background.

As for his wife, it was different. She seemed to expect a matrimony marriage. She did not view forced marriage as an act against her will. It was like she never knew that she had the right to make her own decisions. She doubted that life would improve if people loved and respected each other. She thought that was the basic foundation of marriage. Still, she expected him to fix everything for her and their child. Uncle Serei tried to stay a good father and husband, but his anger and resentment about choices he didn't make took a toll on him. He couldn't move forward with his life as long as he held on to those feelings. Instead, he called it quits after having another daughter and after bringing them to America. He began again without explaining to his daughters the reason he could not give the kind of love that they deserved. Perhaps he did not want to pass on historical trauma to them. Or perhaps, the only way he could live was to abandon his past.

Unlike Uncle Serie, Mom's other brother, Uncle Veasna, whose name meant Lucky in English did not consider the marriage under the Khmer Rouge legitimate. The absence of family and legal documentation, in his view, was not acceptable. How could he even consider it was real when tradition allowed his parents' stamp of approval? The fact that the Khmer Rouge forced him against his will to consummate under the watching eyes of Angka was cruelty enough. He did not invest any emotion in the arraignment. He was seventeen when the Khmer Rouge took over.

Once Cambodia was no longer under the control of the Khmer Rouge, Veasna abandoned the wife and the child at once.

One would think that Uncle Veasna was heartless. However, could you blame him for wanting to be free? He was forced to procreate against his will. It was enough that he had to perform hard labor with limited nutrition. The ultimate cruelty was to have him consummate under pressure. As a city kid, he knew his rights were violated. However, it was not the same if one grew up in rural areas without choice and understanding of human rights. They had to do things because they were told to. For him, it was not enough. Being incarcerated for three years and eight months was enough for him to want to move on without being reminded of the Khmer Rouge. However, twenty years later, he provided support for his daughter in finding happiness in America.

Uncle Serei never found purpose in his life. It was only the moments of satisfaction that he had through multiple relationships and three other children. He never dealt with his trauma. Quick fixes like alcohol and work were just short-term to pass the time, but they never healed the internal wound. Uncle Serei has had multiple jobs since coming to America. The only work that brightened his eyes was being the Bus Driver for the Long Beach Transit. He was so good at what he did that he got multiple Awards for Safety while operating public transportation. Later, I met many Cambodian passengers who spoke highly of him, praising his good attitude and character. I knew Uncle Serei the best because I helped co-sign for some of his cars. Sadly, the trauma he experienced caused him to ignore his health. He was too tired to keep going and didn't want to be a burden to others if he couldn't take care of himself. Therefore, he chose not to care for himself. Uncle Serei passed away in 2018 at the age of sixty-three. At his funeral, I found out about the stress and the feeling of abandonment from his older daughter, which the Khmer Rouge forced him to create without his consent. I felt so bad for her. I wondered whether her judgment of him would change if she knew how hard it was for him to navigate life in a new country after being persecuted emotionally, mentally, and physically.

I was curious about how the Khmer Rouge enforced such unusual punishment on young adults. I asked one of the aunts to explain to me what had happened. She was Veasna Khmer Rouge's wife. I was fond of her after such a short meeting. She was friendly and carefree. She grew up in a rural area without political correctness, attitudes, and manners. She was not shy to display her unpolished vocabulary. I found her to be entertaining when she spoke. It was like she had nothing to hide. She was not pretending to be dignified when she was never taught to be one. More importantly, she did not have to belong to any class to know that she was a good person.

"There were about twenty-five men and women. Angka called out your name. You both came forward and took each other's hands. That was it," she said casually. She knew that the chance of her future together was slim. It was an order between life and death. She had to comply. So did he. However, there was no expectation of it to last on either side. I wondered why Uncle Serei's wife expected matrimony. He did his best to bring her and the child to America with him. He had hoped to make it work because he would never abandon his responsibility. Ultimately, trauma was involved in his decision-making. Unlike Veasna's wife, she accepted the consequence of the revolution that forced her at nineteen to procreate. After they parted, she was able to find her own happiness, knowing it was not a real relationship during the Khmer-forced union.

Before the Khmer Rouge, Cambodian society allowed parents to arrange marriages for their children but rarely

116

forced them against their will. Certainly, they were not required to consummate. Parents wanted their children to marry mostly for economic reasons. However, the Khmer Rouge took it upon themselves to experience how different backgrounds played a role in relationships.

Again, I was investigating the motive behind the forced marriage during the Khmer Rouge.

"Did you meet my uncle beforehand?" I asked.

"No," she said.

"They called my name to come forward. They called his name to come forward. It was fixed." She added.

"There was a couple who refused each other and were killed." It was an immediate example of how they had to be with one another by force.

It was interesting to me. If the Khmer Rouge targeted urban residents, what was the rationale behind compelling young adults from cities to marry young adults from rural areas? If rural upbringing was pure and less corrupt, why did they mix them up with procreation? Was it done to punish the city dwellers? Or perhaps, it was done to bring out the best of the rural population who were not exposed to education or the outside world. I did not understand if the Khmer Rouge treated the rural population better than the city people, so why would they think it was to the rural folk's benefit by marrying the city folks? Perhaps culture and prestige sensed that they were hoping to connect.

I knew that Srey's family had better treatment than my family. They had access to food, just because they were born in the countryside. I tried to understand the real reason behind the forced marriage.

Both uncles were twenty and twenty-three in 1978 when they were selected from the group to marry. There was no wedding ceremony. The best part about being Cambodian is the wedding tradition. The outfits, the music, the food, the people, the events of the season. Mom used to say it was at least seven days. If one lived in a small town, the entire town would come together to celebrate to help with building tents for the kitchen, the folk band, and the main hall.

Of course, the Khmer Rouge reduced the wedding ceremony to shaking hands.

"What if you don't consummate?" I asked, wanting to know all the details.

"You can be charged with treason. Secret police patrolled your shed." She spoke. Without further interrogation from me, I thanked her for sharing. It was interesting to me that my uncles found it difficult to speak of the event, whereas it was easier for the partner who was not a city dweller to share their experience willingly. Perhaps he had more to lose than she did. He knew what it was like to be free. How would she regret when she had nothing to be regretted for?

Subsequently, Mom found all four siblings. She also got good news about her mother, son, and other siblings. They fled Cambodia on time and were now living in the United States. The news came from her cousin, Saveoun, who got into the refugee camp in Thailand but had to risk his life coming back so that Mom would get the news. Otherwise, we had no idea where to go from here. Mom and I would not know how to make our journey into the refugee camp. Mom encouraged all her surviving siblings to flee Cambodia as well. For Mom and me, it was not a recommendation. It was about reuniting with my older brother, Virak. No matter how difficult it would be to flee from Cambodia illegally, we had to take our chance for the happiness of being with family members.

Mom did not waste time claiming back her apartment or grandparents' homes, for Cambodia had no future. It was now about my future. I still had time to make up for the years

I lost from being just a kid. Mom would rather start anew in a new country than be reminded of how she lost a husband and three sons.

Refugee Camp

In 1981, we entered the Khao E Dang refugee camp at the border of Thailand. I was happy to see that I did not have to work for food. There were children with which I could play. There was rice, vegetables, canned goods, and steamed fish. The food was enough to go around, so we did not fight over it.

Mom was bilingual in French. She could speak, read, and write. Her skills and abilities were needed to assist the United Nations personnel. Mom was good at not just translating but organizing each section of the camp to ensure safety and the necessity of survival during the transition process. Working kept her from reflecting on her traumatic experience during the Khmer Rouge. I did not recall she took the time to mourn her losses.

Perhaps she worried about my future. It was 1981. I became a teenager. I had no formal education for six years.

Mom said that I could not go to the English as a Second Language class at the camp.

"It's for the adults." She claimed.

"Besides, you cannot learn another language when you have not yet mastered your own." Mom knew that I could still read and write in Khmer at the basic level. She knew that I had lost six years of learning. Indeed, I needed to improve my reading and writing skills. Without formal education in Khmer, I lacked the academic precision on terminologies and honorific languages that was used to distinguish the level of one position title.

Somehow, she got access to some Khmer books. Most of what she left for me to read were folk stories and novels. Every day, I had to write a summary of what I had learned from each story. Since Mom was working most of the time, she didn't notice the spelling mistakes I made. At least I was still able to understand and use the Khmer language. Nonetheless, I was not exposed to history, geography, and biology.

One day, I felt uncomfortable. Mom had already left for work. My body ached for no reason. When I folded our sleeping mat, I saw a red stain. Then, I was in pain in my lower abdomen. I had stained my pants as well. So, I could not go to ask for help.

Fear came upon me. The only thought that came to mind was death. I expected this day would come, considering how many times I escaped death. I sat still on the bamboo carpet, anticipating the end of me. While waiting for Mom, I got a flashback of the brutality and death I witnessed during the Khmer Rouge. Somehow, it was almost normal to die. However, in my circumstances, I did not see the brutality in what happened to my body. I found it difficult to understand the anatomy of being a girl due to a lack of education and preparation.

As the thought of dying came upon me, regret also took over the fact that I had not had enough of the taste of food. Mom worked with United Nation's staff. Her ability to communicate and translate from French to Khmer was helpful to assist many refugees. She was the middle person to assist in providing guidelines to ensure the safety and process of seeking refuge to accepting countries. She often received snacks from foreign staff such as a chocolate bar or dried cookies that she brought for me. My regret would be that I did not have enough of those candy bars. I remained completely still until my mother returned to our tent.

When she finally did, I showed her what happened. She was calm and instructed me what to do.

"I'm not dying?" I asked her in confusion.

"No. You are Pench Kror Momm," she answered. She said that I was coming of age, being a woman. Of course, I had no idea of what it meant to be a woman. I was so used to being a kid. In fact, I was a kid who saw and had been through too much. I was relieved to be in another stage of my life. Yet, I lacked understanding of what it meant as Mom showed me how to be clean. I lost six years of education. Mom had so much on her mind that she dealt with me as the issue arrived. Nevertheless, I experienced my first trauma as I tried to make sense of becoming a woman in the age of war.

Looking back, I am grateful that I had a Mom to tell me what to do in that situation because I could not imagine what it would be like not to have someone guide the process to proper hygiene and put anguish to rest. I wondered if Mak Yay met such challenges growing up in order for her to wish for an education.

Nevertheless, my Mom failed to warn me that discretion was part of coming of age. Somehow, I was proud of myself. Perhaps, reaching the age that I thought I was not supposed to was overwhelming.

One sunny day at the playground, a group of teenagers were playing. They were mostly boys. They were various in age because of their height different. I was astonished for a moment. It had been a while since I saw children playing. There was just one ball, but they passed it around in circle with amazement. I wanted to be included in the group. So, I asked permission to play.

"No" one of the older boys rejected me.

I was not sure why they denied me. It could be because I was a girl. At the same time, I heard someone shouted, "Go away kid." He was annoyed that I interrupted the game. I was offended at the word "kid." How could they insult me without knowing how old I was. Without thinking I replied back.

"I'm not a kid. I'm a woman now." I said it in Khmer as though I earned my right to brag about my coming of age.

There was laughter among the boys. Still, they did not let me play. However, for the next month or so, when I happened to see the boys from that group, they would repeat my words and laugh at me. Later, I found out that I was supposed to keep my growing body discreet.

In the early 1980s, I was a refugee awaiting relocation to the United States.

Coming To America

The goal of coming to America was to reunite with family members. Mom was thrilled to reunite with her first-born son, mother, siblings, and nieces and nephews. Grandma Mak Yay was so relieved to find out that all her five children survived the Khmer Rouge regime. However, she was sad to know the loss of her son-in-law, three grandchildren, and her husband and his family. Mak Yay had been praying to Buddha every single day since April 1975. She believed that her good deeds spared her children.

Mak Yay even forgave her husband, Ros Sok. He chose to spend his time after retirement with the second wife and children. She had no complaint to the culture and norm that allowed men to have multiple families as long as they had the mean. Children usually had arranged marriages chosen by their parents but chose their own spouses after their parents passed away. I wondered how common it was. I questioned why educated adult children did not challenge existing norms or discuss personal matters openly. Was absolute obedience considered a standard expectation within society? Such expectations caused disastrous outcomes for my generation. It certainly upset Mak Yay, though she took it gracefully. She focused all of her energy on her children instead of dwelling on her personal relationship. She knew that the women in her generation, especially those who came from the countryside received little respect from society. Perhaps, it was the reason that she ensured that her children would be educated so they would have better choices in life.

Nevertheless, Mak Yay upheld her dignity by diligently caring for all ten children. She found joy through watching the success of her children. It was her wish to see the world through learning. She never expected to see America when

Cambodia was in turmoil. Had she not had children who pursued education and established careers, she would not have experienced the outside world. She would not escape the Khmer Rouge. She would not able to live the rest of her life in peace. A young woman from a small town altered her future and that of her descendants by pursuing a fundamental aspiration: becoming literate.

Furthermore, she maintained her commitment to the teachings of Buddha. She sought to forgive others as part of her journey towards achieving inner peace. Her nirvana was all about having her children together and being safe. For Mak Yay, she was always the matriarch of the family. She was surrounded by children, grandchildren, nieces and nephews, monks even neighbors in the days up to her passing in 1996.

It had been thirteen years since I first met Mak Yay. She was waiting for us at LAX when we arrived in Los Angeles for the first time. After eight years and a completely different continent, we were finally able to see each other again. Mom and I were the last ones from our families to arrive in the US. It was in the spring of 1983 that we embraced each other. Tears of joy were more than words could express.

Ironically, it was the spring of 1975 when our entire families were separated. I saw my older brother after eight long years. At least I was relieved to have a brother still. Watching the other three in their final moments was enough for me to last my lifetime.

Meeting my brother Virak initially felt disconnected. His Khmer was limited. My English was at ground zero. It was difficult for us to share the distance of eight years. In addition, I felt a burden in my heart for not being able to provide proof of why our families of seven, including Mom and Dad, were now reduced to three. Only tears could explain why. I was unable to explain my hardship. He was not able to express how lost he was during those years of not knowing what had happened to us.

It was not easier for him either. Arriving in a new country at age ten, alone and without family, he was confused as well. However, he was fortunate to have Mak Yay, Uncles, Aunts, and younger cousins. He strived to navigate a new life independently. The adults were too busy trying to make end meet where the children were left to endure the challenge of being the new kids, the refugee, the children had nowhere else to go. During some occasion when we talked about the past, Virak would tell me he regretted taking that flight out of Phnom Penh, thinking that we would meet soon. If he remained with us, he could assist in ensuring our survival. Perhaps Baron would be alive today. I protested immediately.

"You are the lucky one. If you were to be with us, you might not survive."

Virak wondered if that was the case. Living in America had different challenges. However, he could rely on Mak Yay to provide him with a meal every day after school. It was fate that he escaped the Khmer Rouge untouched.

We settled with my aunt's family. There were over twenty people in the small three-bedroom house with one bathroom. Somehow, there was no complaint. We did not have much in those days, but we seemed so happy together. I remembered how Mak Yay was so creative with food. With one thigh of chicken, she would make a pot of soup.

My brother and young uncles would join the U.S. military after High School one by one. Perhaps they were trying to make room for us newcomers. Or perhaps, to protect and to serve were inherited from our ancestors, regardless of what country we lived in. There was such a great responsibility instilled in all of us.

Mom enrolled me right away in the spring of 1983. I was put into English as a Second Language classes for at least over a year before I was allowed to take regular courses in high school.

At the beginning of high school, I had such a hard time adjusting to regular classes. I was no longer in ESL classes. Therefore, whenever I tried to speak, I would be corrected, or someone would chuckle the correct words for me. I enjoyed learning about other cultures, but I felt intimidated by the confident attitude of the students. When they asked the teacher questions, I saw it as being aggressive because I was experiencing culture shock. I came from a culture where young people were not allowed to express their ideas or opinions. The culture in which direct confrontation was not allowed. We were taught to respect people with titles, ranks, elders, teachers, and those with power and privilege. What happened when there were no check and balance to power? The Khmer Rouge happened.

When I found myself struggling to keep up with others as I learned English, I was disappointed at Mom for not giving me a head start with English at the refugee camp. There were teenagers my age who got their head start the minute they found out that they were going to America. But Mom knew that I had no education since 1975; therefore, the least she could do for me was to remind me that I could still read and write in Khmer. It was not college-level, but it was enough to go by. To her, it was about restoring a sense of self for me. The Khmer language dates back over two thousand years. I could at least read and write before beginning a new language. The only justification she gave me was.

"You can't learn another language when you don't even know your own."

I did not understand what she meant at the time. She never explained properly to me why I had to regain my language skills. Like Mak Yay, Mom had great vision. She knew success would be short-term if one lacked the foundation or root in the planting. What she meant was that having pride in knowing who I was key to rebuilding my life. Language was my ancestral heredity. Language was used to abuse, to kill, to deceive, to love, to be kind, and to be helpful was important to learn. It was my cultural identity.

Knowing my native language allowed me to use the Khmer English dictionary when I did not understand certain words. At the same time, I felt grounded and was willing to continue learning English as I worked my way to become a contributing citizen of the United States.

Even Mak Yay could understand English by watching Wheel of Fortune. I had memories of watching and learning English from that show with Mak Yay as well. I still love the show till today. In fact, one of my bucket lists would be to be on the show. It was a tall wish, but I had hope.

Gradually, I became comfortable with learning English. Graduating from high school after four years was my first step into my educational endeavor. At the same time, I had to work to ensure self-sufficiency.

Mom sewed for a while. Then, her family pitched in to open the Donut Shop so that everyone would have a place to work. It was hard work as I helped clean the trays and mop the floor. But no one complained of hard work because we knew we had worked harder than this a thousand times during the Khmer Rouge. With knowledge of French, it took Mom little time to learn English. She worked at the Donut Shop for longer hours. She named the store "Chez-Moir" in French. It meant "My House." Mom could assimilate into a new culture quickly. Perhaps she wanted to forget her past completely. I was, on the other hand, struggling with how to navigate open environments. I was not used to making my own decisions. Here in America, no one tells you what to do. The freedom of choice was overwhelming.

Mom found her joy in running a small business. One day, a French American man stopped by the store. The name of the shop attracted his attention. He thought it was a French owner. When he entered, he met Mom, a Cambodian refugee who once worked as the head accountant and was now selling donuts and croissants. He was also surprised when Mom spoke French. The divorced, late middle-aged Caucasian man who served in the Korean War was over the moon. He wasted no time courting Mom. They married a year later. I guessed Mom had found her new happiness.

On the other hand, I was not comfortable with the new arrangement. I chose to stay with Mak Yay instead of Mom. Facing puberty, a changing environment, experiencing a cultural gap, and a language barrier, I did not know how to call someone else dad. It was too fast for me to assimilate after what I had been through. Luckily, my stepfather was a bit patient. He had raised children from a previous marriage. I was a challenging teenager with language and cultural gaps that he could mentor.

It was not long before I became comfortable with him. He knew how to connect with me through food. I was amazed as he made Lasagna and Cheesecake. It remains my favorite food of all time.

More importantly, I learned how to be independent from him. I was shy about speaking English, and he made me repeat every word he said to me.

"Practice makes perfect," he said. "Keep on talking. You'll get it one day."

He was right. I kept on practicing. When I stopped focusing on the pronunciation, I was able to say the words correctly.

Life seemed to pass us by when we enjoyed each other as families. My uncles, aunts, and cousins surrounded me. Every weekend, we were together. We did not have much, but it seemed like we had a bundle. We loved having a picnic at the park or at the beach every Saturday.

Five short years went by quickly. My stepfather passed away one evening due to sudden cardiac arrest. Mom and I were with him at the dinner table. We were still eating when he seemed to fall off the chair.

I called 911, and they were instructing us to administer CPR. I did not know what that was at the time. Mom was trying to give him CPR. Unfortunately, the paramedic concluded that he could not be resuscitated. Once again, Mom and I dealt with another loss.

There was also a saying that the good one was taken early. It seemed like that in my family. I wondered if I was bad. Was I being punished by watching loved ones die? The saying of good people goes first and the end-of-life suffering to them did not set, and the end-of-life suffering to them did not sit well with me. Sometimes, I am tempted to be bad just to defy fate. However, deep down, I was guided by morality. The thought of being bad was there, but the action would never happen.

By 1996, Mak Yay ended her life suffering. She was at the last stage of leukemia, where it went undetected for many years. She was the person who would not complain. We could not extend her life. She passed away at the age of seventy-six.

I remained amazed at my maternal Grandma's life. She did well for me and for all my family. Because she had visions, dreams, and hopes, I admired her intelligence and fortitude. For a young woman without a mother early in life, she grew up in a small town to a farmer without access to education, yet she managed to leave a legacy for herself.

Unable to read and write in her own language, she memorized all the Buddhist chanting of solitude, gratitude, blessing, and peace every morning at dawn. I was amazed at this woman who bore children from the ages of eighteen to forty-five. When Mom was having my older brother and me, Mak Yay also had two more sons. She spent over forty-five years having ten children.

In the end, her dreams in life of being educated became all our dreams. If she could see us now, she would be so proud of having granddaughters with noble jobs, such as teachers, librarians, and community educators like me. She would be proud of having granddaughters who earned doctorates, master's, and bachelor's degrees. At the same time, she would be proud of her grandsons having a sense of responsibility when they served in different branches of the U.S. military. Not only did we live by her example, but we became better parents and better citizens. We contribute to society by being kind and considerate to other fellow humans.

Chapter Five
The Impact of Historical Trauma

Anger

I was not aware that anger was both a form of self-protection and a symptom of trauma. I never spent time observing my own feelings until now. I was angry at how the Khmer Rouge came to power. I was angry at the adults for doing little to protect the children. I was angry at most adult survivors for remaining silent after the Khmer Rouge.

I could not accept how the kind and compassionate people turned on one another. I did not understand why children were victims of such atrocity. Why were my brothers and I punished? It was unfair to blame us just because we were born in the city.

I was displeased with the country's leadership during that period. Why did no responsible leaders warn about the society's trajectory? Whatever was great before now is overshadowed with darkness and stained with blood. The statues with kind expressions that I had previously known were now revealed to be deceptive. What happened to centuries of belief in Buddhism of "do no harm to others."

I was confused and disappointed. Whatever progress we made coming into the twentieth century was completely undone. More importantly, I questioned the educated adults in my family and in the society at that period. How was it that they did not have any sense of social responsibility? How was it possible that they went about their professions without considering future consequence for their own children? Was it the blind trust that they had for their political leaders? It was possible because of the culture of respect for authority figures. I remember asking Mom if she ever voted prior to the Khmer Rouge.

"No" she answered.

It seemed like she was unaware of the political circumstances in the country. How was it possible? She was educated. She had a professional job. Yet, she was not adding her voice to ensure the safety and growth of a nation where her five children were the future. It did not make sense to me. Perhaps, the culture of respecting authority without conditions allowed bad actors to change the course of a country.

For example, I grew up hearing about Ta Bromat Bromong (the Khmer version of the Boogeyman). Children disappeared into thin air. Parents warned their children consistently not to wander alone in the city. Children continued to go missing without questions being asked. Why? There was certainly law and order. My maternal grandfather was a retired customs agent. Apparently, there was an abduction of children. Why wasn't there a national outrage? Instead, the adults continued to tell the story as though it were a folk tale instead of a real event. Indeed, it was a real event. Mom said that the Khmer Rouge soldiers were trained to be ruthless and cunning. They had no sense of humanity. It was like they were there to just follow orders. They were not commissioned to think for themselves.

To me, the Khmer Rouge was nonsensical. It did not make any sense for good people to act so viciously on their own people. I was disappointed at the adults for not doing enough to allow such an event to happen in the twentieth century. When I met the adults who claimed that the Cambodian society prior to the Khmer Rouge was progressing and at its best. I wondered what filter they used to only see the good and the best. Because if things were all good, then the Khmer Rouge would never have happened. I would never lose my childhood and family members. I wanted the adults in that generation to take some responsibility for their actions and inactions. How was it possible that no one with common sense did anything to influence the top and allowed such destruction to occur in the home that they loved?

For instance, Mom's great-aunt was the best in the community for being the first woman to be Chief of Medicine, a professor at the school of medicine in Cambodia. She was known as Madam Tith Morn. Her noble husband did well for the country. They were the best couple of their time. They were able to flee to France with two small sons prior to the Khmer Rouge. Yet, when Sihanouk proposed a return of all knowledgeable people to join hands with the Khmer Rouge to rebuild the country, they returned blindly because of their honorable commitment to Sihanouk. They had no idea that they had left their children to be orphans. They were captive and eventually killed once they returned safely to Cambodia's land. Her picture is still hung at the Toul Sleng Museum today.

How could they trust without verification? How did they succeed at the expense of others' suffering? Why didn't they question their leaders about fairness and justice for all? How was it possible to see nothing and to do nothing if they were among good people? How could the right thing be wrong if they were to step up to help others with children who went missing? I had many questions. I wanted to know whether the adults in that generation had any social responsibilities. Apparently, they had children. Shouldn't they want to carve an environment that is conducive for their children to grow?

My brothers and I did nothing wrong, yet we paid an enormous price. My three brothers paid with their lives. I paid with emotional and mental pain for the rest of my life. In addition, I was angry at the adults who chose to save themselves rather than the children. I knew that Baron could have lived if he had received a spoon of rice porridge after his body was rid of the bacteria that gave him diarrhea. Mom said she traded her last jewelry, the wedding ring that she hid by sewing it inside her bra. She was trading for a spoon of rice, yet a lady who was the go-between stole it for herself. How selfish of her? I thought. What happened to "thou shall not steal"? Wasn't it "Kone Ott-Pooch?" The term referred to no ancestry connection when one became a thief. There was no gentleness, kindness, dignity, or morality. People only looked out for the number one, self.

Without knowing that I had trauma, I often got mad at my sons for little reason. For example, I was mad at them for not finishing the food on their plates. I was mad at them for being wasteful. I was mad at them for being picky about what they should eat. In my view, I assume that as long as proper nutrients being given, they should appreciate without hesitation.

Sometimes, I recalled saying to my sons, "You would not survive if you were in the Khmer Rouge."

I remember being mad at my parents during the Khmer Rouge for not preparing me to face evils in the world. I saw countless wrongdoings without remorse or consequence. I was shocked by the realization of karma. Didn't they feel that there would be consequences for their actions? If it was not justice, what about ethics and morals? Somehow, I was channeling my trauma to my children, thinking that they needed to be prepared in case what had happened to me might happen to them.

Then, I realized that I fled Cambodia to find safety to raise children so that they would not have the men who made the tragedies that I had to experience. Therefore, why would I create fear for them? They deserved to see the world with a positive outcome. Nevertheless, I had to ensure that they did it by being aware of my experience so that they could be sensitive to what I went through without thinking how abnormal I was in my view of the world sometimes.

Although oversharing could be humorous, I told my young sons that I ate crickets and other bugs during the Khmer Rouge. I owe crickets my life for the little protein they provided me with.

One day, playing in the backyard, my son, Baron who was six years old at the time, was excited to give it to me. It was a great gift. Perhaps it was my life savoir that he wanted me to keep.

"Mom, Mom, look at what I've found." He closed both palms together, hiding something inside.

"Look! Cricket. I found it. Eat it. Eat it, Mom, you used to eat it." It was daring. Certainly, he did not remember the fact that I had to eat it to survive. For him, it was interesting.

"Why should I? There is tastier food in our fridge."

"Aww!" He was disappointed. He wanted to witness something unusual. He tried to see whether what I said was true or not. I insisted that he put the cricket back where he found it.

It would not taste the same if I were to eat it just to show off to my kid. I was hoping to convey the message that, in desperation, survival was key regardless of edible insects. However, when we are no longer in danger, we should be grateful to that insect and allow them to be free without adding casual side dishes for humans to consume.

Interestingly enough, when I visited Cambodia a few times, I saw different types of insects becoming street snack food. I wondered if people were still living in poverty or if it had become acceptable to be included in human consumption. I thought about other living things that relied on bugs for their food. Would they have enough if humans found it was acceptable to enjoy crickets now and then?

In addition, I was confused when Mom got angry at me, and she slapped me so hard on my cheek. I was already twenty-one. I was in college, bridging into mainstream America. I excelled in accounting and tried to understand how the economy works.

To her, having versatile of skills would be helpful one day, like she passed for being a seamstress during the Khmer Rouge because she knew how to make clothes. She was mad because I had no interest in sewing the way she did. She attempted multiple times to teach me how to sew. I failed and I refused to do it. I preferred reading all kinds of books, except sewing and needlepoint.

She tried to motivate me to learn how to sew by suggesting that it would be economical for me in the long run.

"You can save lots of money when you have kids one day." She made all of my dresses.

"A woman should know how to sew." She nagged. She was also being stereotype about women. I did not expect that from her. It was obvious that growing up as the oldest of ten children, she had to do many things to help her mother. She learned to make clothes for her siblings. She helped her mother cook. She had to get good grades in school. She was the role model for her younger siblings. Mom was taught to work hard and to be versatile in her skills.

By this time, I was indoctrinated into the American's ideology. I did not have to know many things to be sufficient. I just needed to learn how to use my skills and time effectively. The idea that a woman had to know many things to support a household was no longer irrelevant in the twenty-first century. I attempted to give her my comparable cost analysis.

"It is more productive for me to focus on the thing that I'm good at. It is efficient to just buy the thing that I need without having to do it myself." I explained along those lines that Mom slapped me.

She was angry. She was stunned. In her generation, she could never speak back to her parents in that manner. Yet, I did. She felt betrayed, thinking that I owed her my life just because she gave birth to me and brought me all the way to America. Without another word, she left the room. I was angry as well. I was speechless at her action. I also proceeded to my room. I did not come out to eat dinner. I was protesting Mom's action. I was on a hunger strike. Since I had been in the state, I enjoyed the luxury of having three meals a day. To decline one meal was an incredible sacrifice. Yet, I had to show Mom that I was disappointed in her actions.

Mom never apologized for slapping me. In her mind, she thought that it would benefit me. Perhaps, she anticipated another Khmer Rouge, and I could survive by being able to alter clothes for others. It was a favor that she kept herself alive. It was tough for her to let go of the past. The experience taught her to be prepared. On the other hand, I was younger. I was able to navigate life by just working hard and being determined to succeed. I knew my flaw, and it was okay. I forgave Mom because she acted on her trauma. It never happened again.

Shame

I did not realize that I experienced trauma when I adopted my new country quickly. It was all about forgetting the past. The eagerness to assimilate was to deny the emotional and mental impact of the atrocities. I did not want to be known as a Cambodian refugee. Luckily, California was the State that had the most diverse Asian Americans in the Country. I was happy to be invisible.

I maintained a healthy denial for a long time. I was even ashamed of who I was and where I came from. I was ashamed to be in the same ethnic group as people who destroyed the livelihood of children. Even though I was a victim, I felt a sense of moral obligation to those who minimized their ethics just to be in a group or just to look out for themselves, never mind how others suffered. I wondered how they lived with themselves. I thought we, the descendants of Khmer Angkor, had a certain pride to maintain. The thought of abandoning what were rights was despicable.

Somehow, in my twenties, I was not ready to face my past. As I became involved in the workforce and continued schooling, I met quite a lot of people. Without asking direct questions, people seemed to assume and spoke to me in Vietnamese or Tagalog. I used to stay quiet and walk away without correcting their mistakes. Sometimes, when people thought that I was an immigrant rather than a refugee, I just accepted it as well. I knew that being a refugee was more severe than being an immigrant. Being an immigrant, one came to the country by choice to seek betterment for one's future. However, being a refugee, one had no choice but to leave their hometowns due to dangerous circumstances that left them with emotional and mental wounds. To accept that I was a refugee was to admit that I was broken emotionally and mentally.

More importantly, I felt ashamed of my last name, Pol. I was afraid of what people would think of me as related to Pol Pot, especially when I came across Cambodian families.

Survivor Guilt

Survivor's guilt is the primary obstacle to the progress I have made in my new country. At times, I felt a profound sense of responsibility to achieve more and aspire higher due to the reality that I survived while others did not. Other times, I felt frozen and numb, preventing me from achieving any goals.

The fact that I avoided death countless times, made me became aware of how precious my life is. At the same time, I felt such a burden to be living. I felt guilty when I indulged myself too much. I felt guilty when I ate too much. I held back from enjoying the plentiful good food around me. Somehow, I thought that living was good enough. There was no need to splurge.

More often, I witnessed survivors who accepted the bare minimum or the basic needs due to the guilt. They lacked the drive to improve.

Conversely, I witnessed survivors who never had enough. They kept on striving to achieve mostly materials to fulfill that hollow space which seemed to exist after they went through such an ordeal. For many survivors, immediate gratification seemed to work. It worked briefly.

At the same time, I witnessed countless survivors used their spirits of humanity to do good things for others in the community. I was among them for thinking that my appreciation of this life was to do good for others as a way to thank the invisible force for allowing me to live and experience the changes in society, country, and the world.

Meanwhile, I inherited skepticism, fear, defensiveness, and sensitivity from the Khmer Rouge. I did not think that was trauma from my childhood experience. I thought it was just being smart to keep up the shield because I had no idea when such an event would strike again. At the same time, I would feel that if I had to leave, I might as well take nothing for granted, even if I lived for a day. The impact of such traumatic history stayed in the mind and was displayed in the behaviors. The reason I did not indulge in such traumatic behavior was that I felt some guilt for living. I felt a sense of responsibility to keep the memories of my brothers alive.

Somehow, I was the only proof that they existed at one point in their young lives. It was a burden to remember. Yet, I saw no other choice.

When I witnessed so many survivors giving up their lives easily because they did not want to fight anymore, I felt ashamed of them. I thought that they forgot about how courageous they were to live through such horrific times. At the same time, I felt that the burden in their heart was too much to bear. They called it quits by failing to take care of their physical and mental health. I could not imagine their unspoken pains.

I witnessed adult survivors, including my mom's aunt, give up on life after surviving the Khmer Rouge, only to pass away easily in America. Her name was Som Bok. She passed away at the age of sixty-two from refusing to get treatment for her diabetes. Som Bok vowed never to go hungry again. She would eat whatever she desired without considering what it would do to her physical health after finding out that she had diabetes. It was like she had no willpower to refuse food. It was a controllable disease if she practiced some restraint by eating less white rice or sweets. She did not think that her life was worth it any longer. Perhaps she was just too tired to live. It was such a burden to live with what she had been through. She lost her husband, dignity, property, and country. For her, she had no children to feel obligated that she needed to live for them.

In addition, Mom's cousin, Saveoun Ven, survived the Khmer Rouge, yet he made careless judgments when it came to his own life. All he wanted for himself was to represent the good spirits of humanity. He sacrificed his life to be a monk since he was fifteen. The kindness, compassion, and honor he lived by were commendable. However, when the Khmer Rouge took over, he had to abandon monkhood to work in the field as required. His dream and life changed after he persevered during the Khmer Rouge. Coming to

America with limited skills, he worked in maintenance in the casino. He got married and had one son. He achieved his American dream of owning a home by living below the poverty line, my choice so that he could save enough to purchase a house. He even failed to buy proper medication for his asthma that he developed through working in the smoking environment every day in the late 1980s and early 1990s before smoking was banned from casinos. Without proper medication and treatment for asthma, he stopped breathing one day. He died in 2010 due to respiratory complications. When I spoke to his son, all he wanted was to have a father for comfort. Or perhaps Uncle Soveoun felt the pressure of survivor's guilt that he assumed dying would be better than living. In survivor's guilt, I noticed that we do not value ourselves. We did not place importance on ourselves.

As for me, I also used to feel guilty for living. I filled my time with work and school, and a job that focused on others so that I avoided focusing on myself. Deep down, I still asked the question, Why me? Why couldn't my brothers Baron, Varin, and Phirum survive? They would have done great things in life. They had a purpose. They had dreams. The Khmer Rouge took away all their potential to be great.

I, on the other hand, just wanted to be a little girl. I would've played all day if I could have. I enjoyed the attention from my father, who had all-boys siblings until his Mom adopted a girl. To have me and four boys, Dad was on top of the world with his family achievement. He worked hard to support his family. He also put the family first at all costs.

That final day, when he visited us after Phirum and Varen died, I saw a man without hope. He was broken into many pieces. His physical condition showed that he did not have long to live. Yet, he pushed himself to walk and talk as though his spirit guided him to us for the last goodbye. It was like he took a photographic memory with him as he returned to his labor camp.

I remember hearing my brothers talk about their ambitions at such young ages. They knew what they wanted to do when they grew up. To witness their dreams, perishing along with them, left me broken for life.

Varen was destined to be in the medical field. He aspired to join the medical field. According to my parents, Varen was unique. He was always overly organized and well-prepared. He treated his utensils like surgical scalpels. He would wash them after each meal with hot water and store them separately from others so that no one could pass on any germs. He did the same with his toothbrush. He had a special place to store his own hygiene products.

Baron declared at age seven that he would join the Marines. He wanted to be a commander just like his uncle, his mom's brother-in-law. He adopted the marine code of conduct that modeled bravery, honesty, and compassion. He demonstrated those characteristics when he stood up for me and others during the time when people told their children to look out for themselves to survive.

Finally, I remember my youngest brother, Phirum. He was only six years old when he died. He had such a big heart. He had the magic touch of a healer. He loved our family dog. When the dog was sick, he nursed it back to life. When Phirum was sick, our dog would not step outside of the house until Phirum recovered. The bond he had with animals and humans earned him a reputation for being soft and compassionate. He would have been the best veterinarian if he were alive.

Our family dog's name was Tropp. The pronunciation of "Tropp" could mean either wealth or eggplant. Mom would correct me as "wealth," while my brothers and I would agree with "eggplant" as the definition of how the name meant to us. We were more plane was humble to us. It was devastating to all of us to witness Tropp getting shot as we evacuated our home on that fateful day of April 17, 1975. I did not think Phirum ever recovered from that ordeal.

When I remembered my brothers, I wanted to do more for them and for my life, and I wanted to live for them as well. I've come to understand it was my survivor's guilt.

In addition to anger, shame, and guilt, I became paranoid.

When I watched January 6 on TV, my heart raised a million beats. My thoughts of divisiveness could lead to the Khmer Rouge. I began to have a panic attack. I assumed all kinds of things might happen. I even updated my suitcase to include recent pictures of my sons. I had an emergency suitcase on standby in case I had to run on short notice. Or perhaps, in a fire or some other crisis, I would have something to last for a while.

At the same time, when the COVID-19 pandemic began, I prepared each day like it was my last day. Suddenly, my body tricked me into having all kinds of symptoms. I would Google my symptoms to see the possibility of any tie to the COVID-19 variant. I spent money on the test each time I felt that I had one symptom just to have peace of mind. It was all negative, of course. I evaluated my own condition every time I had acid reflux, chest pain, and body aches as a sign of a heart attack or stroke. I was obsessed with dying just because fears triggered trauma.

Knowing that trauma does exist within me, I avoided most news. I was able to keep myself occupied with what was important to me. When I had free time, I would binge-watch period dramas. I have learned to soften my scar by simply avoiding news that might trigger my paranoia.

Parenting

In my thirties, I knew that I wanted to have a family and children. However, I did not anticipate that trauma would overshadow my ability to think clearly while trying to protect my child.

In my culture, when a young woman is in her thirties, she is considered an old maid. I was so glad that I had an educated mother. She never pushed me to have a relationship for the sake of the biological clock. I got to experience being independent.

I was working full-time while attending school at night. I was ambitious about learning. I explained to Mom about why I should move out to live on my own near work and school. Mom was against the idea at first. I provided a detailed explanation regarding the risks associated with driving at night. I calculated the time I would save for work, school, and rest. What I said made sense to her. She understood that I worked hard to be independent. She also had to overcome the cultural belief that a young woman shouldn't live outside her home before marriage. Of course, while Mom allowed me to be on my own, she got lots of criticism from her relatives.

"What if something happened to her?" her male cousin protested. Mom did not allow fear to overshadow the important path that I chose for myself. The least she could do for me was to trust my judgment.

It was a great experience for me to be on my own. After I completed a graduate degree and spent over six years in one job, I was able to seek other challenges. Moving from the public sector to the private sector, I learned and met many challenges. I kept on trying out new organizations until I felt that I was at home. It was working for the Cambodian community organization that I felt belonged. Somehow, I felt that I had a purpose in my work. I was on my way to a meaningful journey.

One day, Mom asked me to join her volunteer group in the Long Beach community. Most people in her group were older, like her generation, except one. He came from a Chinese Cambodian background. I still harbored my prejudice toward the Chinese Cambodian men. I swore during the Khmer Rouge that I was not marrying one. I saw how selfish and lacking no manners even as children. No way, I would not even consider the Chinese Cambodian heredity to be in the options for my future mate.

He was the only single one in the group of older adults. He was rude, obnoxious, egotistical, and possessed an unconventional worldview. Even though, like me, schooled in America, he would not change the way he learned from childhood. I assumed that he was just like those kids that I met during the Khmer Rouge. I wondered what had happened to all of them.

To my surprise, he asked me out. I said "No" many times. Yet, he persisted. Finally, I gave in because he was genuine in his feelings. We got married within a year.

There was a saying in Khmer, "Sa-Op-Jom-Pop-Ler."

It meant in the same way as never say never.

I believe in this karma. I examined my own bias and realized that I assumed a person's character based on their background. Due to my past traumatic experiences, I was unable to recognize an individual as I had preconceived notions about their ethnicity. Once I understood that a person's value is independent of their background, I was able to accept them. Marriage is about good timing and choice. I was ready to settle down. I chose to love my husband.

We were totally opposites from one another. Yet, we had the courage to face our differences. As a result, we bring out the best in each other. If I did not make that choice I would not know the devotion and commitment we had for one another.

Anyhow, Mom was thrilled. She loved planning the traditional Cambodian wedding. I delegated all the wedding planning to Mom. She had to get the perfect folk music. The evening Buddhist Blessing ceremony, the photo, and the flower, while I was a participant.

In our culture, the wedding is for parents. We agreed to give the parents the joys of watching us start a new life together. However, the Cambodian wedding was also to honor and thank our parents for their upbringing of us.

The wedding ceremony included the groom's procession where the groom's side brought food and gifts as a gesture of good faith. It was like you never go to a person's house without bringing anything. As for the wedding, you were expected to bring many gifts if you were the groom's family. It was a great tradition because all the food and gifts would be shared with all in attendance.

From the bride's family to enter for the special day to begin. The meaning of the music and each step itself gave me joy. For our friends, who had not been to a Cambodian wedding before, the experience was intriguing.

The song and dance provided instruction for each step of the process as well. I always wondered why the song was so emotional. It was emotional for the parents who reached this gratification stage of seeing their children's marriage. The song called out angels and ancestors to witness and bless the commitment of the new couple as they embark on their journey together.

The song was sung in Khmer. It was so moving that I could not stop crying. I thought about my father, brothers, and grandparents. I wished they could see me and bless me as I moved on to the next chapter of my life. I was sad because my father was not around to share this precious moment with me. Tears kept falling from my eyes without me being able to stop them. I couldn't hold back the tears, and they washed away all my makeup. Some relatives were whispering words of superstition about crying at a wedding. It was considered bad luck. I did not care. I was just wishing that my father could see me at that moment.

The best part of the Cambodian wedding ceremony was the wedding costumes. The colorful silks included the traditional *Kben*. The outfit began with *Kben* to *Sarong Bott* at the end of the wedding ceremony.

The ancient Khmer people were highly intelligent. Mak Yay used to say that centuries ago, young women wore *Kben* to protect themselves from men. It took great effort to know how to put on the *Kben*. It took great effort to take it off as well. Young women before marriage had to wear it. It was used like a chastity belt but to protect women.

During the Angkor period, any type of material could be used for *Kben*. Nowadays, *Kben* is only used for special occasions, such as classical dance performances or a wedding. Silk is the appropriate material to use for special occasions. The Kben is made from silk fabric that is three to five yards long. When wearing the Kben, a woman centers herself in the fabric, wrapping the silk around both of her legs. She starts by tying the top with a knot near her belly button, then rolls and spins the rest of the fabric to create the "tail." The tail is brought between the legs and is tucked back into the fabric at the top. A *Kben* is not only fabric but also a belt, usually gold in color; the belt wraps across the top of the *Kben,* securing it in place. The belt is tight, tight in order to keep everything in place, to make sure nothing comes undone. As the belt secures, the tail is untucked and is wrapped around the belt, under, around, and through. The *kben* looks almost like a pair of poofy shorts, but it represents control, knowledge, and beauty. It is impossible to get undone in a short period of time. Should there be unexpected harm to a woman, she had time to call for help.

The last of the outfits included a silk Sarong. It had no control at the bottom. It signified a married woman.

Why has Cambodian history lost its purpose? Why did *Kben* become known to the royal court only? Something with historical meaning and purpose should be taught throughout not just groups with privileges.

At least people continued to honor the wedding tradition. At the same time, they should learn the importance of families and history, not just for the sake of wearing night outfits.

The wedding was such a special occasion that we had families and friends who came from other States as well. We reserved thirty tables for three hundred guests. Somehow, we had almost four hundred guests for the evening receptions. Tables were added immediately. Cambodian weddings were always inaccurate because there was no RSVP. As of today, they have learned to RSVP because food is expensive.

We have been married for twenty-five years, and we're blessed with two amazing sons. When my firstborn was ten months old, I took a trip out of the State for a family wedding.

I had flown before, but never with a baby. This time, I paid close attention to the flight attendant who gave emergency instructions. Afterward, I was confused, irritated, and angry.

"Why?" I murmured to myself. Trying to recall what she had said. I kept hearing, "When the oxygen mask drops, make sure to put it on yourself first before assisting a minor."

I was dumbfounded. My mother instinct would first place the oxygen mask onto my child. I could not comprehend its meaning. How could I prioritize myself? I even thought that the instruction was not culturally appropriate. Perhaps it was the American way?

I was in agony trying to understand the emergency instructions. It was twenty years later, when I went back to school, that I found out that my worldview was being distorted due to trauma. In my case, relating to my son while flying.

It was like something came over me and not allowing me to see clearly. All of my thoughts went to my child. When I heard the word emergency, I related it to the crisis. I would sacrifice myself if my son lived. All I could think was my child. I was irrelevant to his survival.

It was until I went back to school when I realized that I did not think it through. Critical thinking plays a significant role in education. It helped me to realize that I was wrong.

I forgot that if Mom had died during the Khmer Rouge, where would I be? If she had been willing to risk her life just to save mine, where would I be now? Just by asking these two questions, I became overwhelmed. I realized I would never have made it to America. I would never have escaped the jungle. I would probably become a slave to the Khmer Rouge men running in hiding after the war. I was the lost child; no one knew that I was still alive. Would I still be alive if Mom had not asked for the whereabouts of the woman she served as a seamstress? Will I be able to experience milestones such as driving a car, earning academic degrees, contributing to the community, positively impacting others, getting married, raising two sons, and reuniting with my brother? I realized that I was not thinking critically about the emergency instruction. I was thinking with fear in mind.

Parenting was about giving directions and guidance to a child. If I refused to put it on myself first and put it on my son instead, I would die, and eventually, he would die, too.

My need to shield my sons from any dangers was the trigger of my trauma. Instead of using common sense, I was willing to sacrifice my life for his well-being. I did not think he would survive without me. How did I assume a child could exist without proper love and care?

Suddenly, I remember a time in the Khmer Rouge where Mom persevered to live to ensure that I would find her. When she was sick and could not fetch me from the children's camp, she placed herself in the direction where I would walk by. It was not a coincidence. Mom used her mother's instinct to ensure that we would meet if each of us was still alive.

It was my mother who got me out of the Khmer Rouge's control province, even after the liberators occupied the city. It was Mom who orchestrated our journey across the border to find family members. It was Mom who shaved my hair to get rid of lice and to make me look like a boy at thirteen to avoid being raped by pirates of the jungle. How did I forget that the reason I was still alive was because of her? The determination of a mother to bring about a better future for her daughter. How did I forget when Mom dragged me by the hair, crossing a river where we both could not swim?

The emergency instruction was not as culturally inappropriate as I thought; it was common sense about the rule of nature. The young needed the old to guide, love, nurture, and care.

Chapter Six
My View of the Causation

How can I come to terms with historical trauma without fully understanding the causation? There had to be reasons why ordinary people inflicted pain on one another. When I heard adult victims speak of the Khmer Rouge, they made it sound like the Khmer Rouge were not Khmer. Yet, all the Khmer Rouge and their supporters were all Khmer. They happened to be living in the rural areas and countryside to retain access and privilege versus a family like mine being forced out of our home in the pretext of temporary government reorganization of the cities. How was it possible that the adults failed to anticipate the plan to eradicate certain types of people?

At least, I understood that the root of evil was within us, waiting to come out to be the executors and guards. I only knew that the Khmer people were just like my Mak Yay, kind and compassionate with a deep belief in Buddhism. And how each day, she meditated to achieve "Vajra," which was the force to break through obstacles and cultivate the mind. It was to strengthen the inner spirit.

To witness the breakdown of a society and see the good turn into bad was still shocking to me. I wondered what made people lose their ability to comprehend between right and wrong. What made them do what they did?

It still breaks my heart when I think about how I lost my three brothers. I also feel deep sadness knowing I never got the chance to learn from my three grandparents, how they were raised, what their lives were like, and what shaped them into the people they became. It feels so wrong that older people are often treated as if they don't matter anymore, just because they can't work or contribute in the same way to the economy. They still have so much wisdom and value. When did the village Khmer Rouge leader think only about capital gains and never mind about those who contributed to the success? All I learned from the Khmer Rouge was about the benefit to the State, and the human aspect was just a casualty. At the same time, it was not just about production. It was about treating city dwellers in the most unbearable ways so that they would die painfully on their own. It was the treatment of such disdain and inhumaneness that was difficult for me to forget. I was left confused and angry at the behaviors of the adults during that time. I accepted the civil war and its destruction to the country, but the ill-will behaviors toward one another were at a different level. It was not just a casualty because of the changing course of a new government, but it was an act of revenge and hatred.

After collecting information and assessing personal experiences from myself, other adults, and educational materials, I observed significant dissatisfaction due to exploitation, neglect, and historical inequality.

The Khmer Rouge used the weakness of its own people to advance its political agenda. They did it by giving power to those who had never had power before. They gave the power to individuals who had no exposure to education to understand that power came with responsibility. There was no guard rail to the power given to those to discipline others. Therefore, even children were not spared from persecution. The result of unchecked power was deadly. The violence against city residents was unjustifiable, considering the consequences of each action.

Education

It took over forty years and a continued education to make sense of what had happened to me and my family. I have lived in denial long enough to protect my sanity. Now, I have found some peace by accepting historical trauma. I want to mend my heart with a thread of information. I want closure to the internal wound deep down in my subconscious.

I managed to live over half a century because I was able to craft the perfect band-aid or numb it with antiseptic. The wound remained hidden deep within me. When minor challenges in life arrived, sometimes, I overreacted or retreated in sadness, believing that my hard work did not change human behavior like those I had seen in the past. The negative emotion got the best of me. Simultaneously, my body experienced a convulsion, making it challenging for me to maintain regular breathing. Fear became my dark shadow. Common-sense decisions became blurry.

How can a child like me be normal after seeing and experiencing such brutality? How can I use my pain to be a lesson in humanity? What had happened in the Khmer Rouge was an act of rebellion in the worst ways. The least I could do was trying to understand why. Perhaps it was the only way that I could ease my pains of loss.

John Dewey once said, "Education must be conceived as a continuing reconstruction of experience." Indeed, for me, education is the tool to connect the past, present, and future. Moreover, it helps me to find purpose in life. I am fortunate to believe that I can mend my broken heart with knowledge. At the same time, I am inspired by my grandmother's wish. Mak Yay wanted to be literate and educated in order to make informed decisions for herself. Even though she could not achieve such a dream during her generation, she ensured that her children had the opportunity that she was not afforded. At least she knew what she wanted, even though she could not choose to say no to a marriage arrangement. My Mak Yay inspired me to have the dream of literacy for future generations.

However, her dream was crushed during the Khmer Rouge revolution, when education was deemed the cause of corruption. How could that be? Mak Yay worked so hard to leave the quiet provincial life behind for the big city, where she had to learn the rules of law and the manners that came with it when she married into an educated family. She gave birth to thirteen children; ten survived passed infancy, three college graduates with successful careers, one in medical school, three in high school, and three in elementary school. To think that her efforts were deemed wicked was to lose all consciousness.

The Khmer Rouge sought to destroy humanity in itself when it used the largest population, who did not get to be refined, to do their dirty work. The Khmer Rouge manipulated the rural population, who did not get to learn their own language, culture, history, and humanity. They did not know that communication could solve problems. They did not learn that trust can be verified. In short, they believed that they were the victims of society, which neglected their needs for the betterment of the top ten percent. The injustice and disparity permitted them to seek retribution. These were the people who were not able to access education and health care. Therefore, they became resistant to the rule of law. They were good people who became hopeless. People without hope would do anything to get ahead. Indeed, the Khmer Rouge succeeded in turning the uneducated and uncultured individuals into unintentional killers.

Plato once said, "Ignorance is the root and stem of all evil."

After the Khmer Rouge, I often heard from many Cambodian adults who said, "Ignorance is bliss." I could not comprehend why they would think so. Then, I realized that those who believed in "ignorance is bliss" had all of their family members intact. At the same time, I lost two-thirds of my family.

This statement used to bother me. I even got offended. I also got skeptical about whether those who survived with their families were part of the Khmer Rouge.

At one point, I blamed my parents for being educated. I thought perhaps my father and three brothers would still be alive if they were living in rural areas without an education. I thought perhaps my grandparents got to live their lives throughout their golden years, allowing me to learn more about what it was like for them growing up in early 1900s Cambodia. Or I thought that I would suffer less if I had not been born into an educated working-class family in Phnom Penh. At the same time, I knew if Mak Yay knew my thoughts, she would be disappointed. She spent her life dedicating herself to ensuring that her children would be better than her. How could I wish to undo her hope and dream?

My thought was wrong. I should not envy adults who survived the Khmer Rouge without education. Because even when they got to start their lives over again in a free country, many of them failed to see the opportunity for themselves and for their daughters. I knew of many teenage Cambodian girls my age who did not get to graduate from high school or go on to college because their parents wanted them to get married. It was the life that they knew for young girls. They used culture and tradition to maintain their identities even though the environment was different. I felt sorry for some of the girls who could not say no to their parents.

For this reason, I appreciated the educational background of my mother. She never forced her cultural beliefs about marriage on me. Instead, she let me make my own choices in this new country. In fact, she pushed me to stay in school, even though learning English was hard, let alone going after a college degree. Little by little, I made progress in school while working full-time to support myself. I was given the freedom to take control of my life and become independent.

Mom understood the value of freedom and opportunity. She did not allow our grievance to overshadow the opportunity for us to live life with purpose. As a result, I believe that education is a necessity for everyone. Perhaps cultivating the human spirit of never submitting to evil by understanding basic human rights would make our world a better place.

I believe that if we are informed about the past without being afraid of politics or bias, we can learn not to repeat history ever again.

Based on my current knowledge, I passionately believe in the importance of education for a nation's development. Learning from the past, however uncomfortable, strengthens the future. I could only imagine a better outcome if the French took the time to understand Cambodia's history before bringing in ethnic Vietnamese to work in some key positions during its reign. If the French had focused on helping ordinary Cambodians to enhance the economy, there might have been less disparity in wealth among the rural Indigenous Khmer population. If education was free and accessible to all rural population they would not easily sway by the Khmer Rouge to terminate educated groups for they would be needed to rebuild the country. Self-preservation and the needs to see Cambodia "pure" again with less ethnic minority groups were the goal in turning ordinary Cambodians into killers. It was the fear of annihilation that coerced them to turn on one another without thinking of future consequences.

Leadership

The lack of the right leadership brought Cambodia to its knees. The monarchy that ruled the Khmer Empire since its inception did not pass on the vision, courage, perseverance, and commitment. Instead, I saw poor character traits.

Norodom Sihanouk oversaw Cambodia for over half of a century, yet he was not done wanting to be the most powerful person in Cambodia. Without a doubt, Sihanouk was nothing compared to Jayavarman II, who founded the Khmer Empire and called himself King. Yet, after receiving independence from the French in 1953, Sihanouk called himself the "Father of a Nation." He was popular among elders and women because of his descendants from the thousands of years of royal families. However, there was no evidence of the actual DNA relation to Jayavarman descendants because the King had many wives and concubines, where power struggles were among the secrets of the royal relationship.

Of course, Mom's generation would not speak ill of Norodom Sihanouk. She was taught to respect authority figures even if they had character flaws. Mom seemed so proud when she spoke of the time, she was selected to receive Sihanouk as he visited her school. She noted that wherever he went, music and women were parading alongside him. It was no wonder his entitlement attitude and the craving for power got the best of him.

Sihanouk was furious when the U.S. backed Lon Nol's administration and overthrew his reign of power. He wanted to remain the Head of State of Cambodia forever. While he was exiled in China, he reached out to the Khmer Rouge, his former enemies, and pledged his support to overthrow the Lon Nol government. Sihanouk made a deal with the devil to save his own ego but thought nothing about the people.

The Khmer Rouge promised to reinstate Sihanouk if he advocated for the people to support the new revolution and asked for those who had skills and experience to return home for the purpose of rebuilding the country. Sihanouk did his part as he agreed to broadcast via radio from China, asking people to give their trust to the Khmer Rouge. Sihanouk's statement provided legitimacy for the Khmer Rouge and made people believe that the Khmer Rouge would not harm its own people. There was hope and trust that the internal conflict would finally be resolved. There was no more fighting. Peace was back in Cambodia.

Mom's great aunt, Madam Tith Morn, who had become the first woman to be a Chief physician, fluent in French, teaching young doctors to be the best in their field, returned to Cambodia after safely getting into France to be killed by the Khmer Rouge at Toul Sleng, just because she heard the call for service by Sihanouk. Her picture still hangs on the wall of Toul Sleng today.

Little did they know what the Khmer Rouge was capable of. Military personnel put down their guard because they believed in Sihanouk. Retired law enforcement, such as my grandfathers, on both sides, did not think that their lives and the lives of their children were at risk, including grandchildren. How wrong were they? The deception left them speechless. I am certain if they could go back, they would have done what was possible to protect their families and country from such madmen. The opportunity to die with honor was taken away from them because of a man they believed to be "the father of a nation."

Once Sihanouk returned to Cambodia, the Khmer Rouge did not give him full power. He was under house arrest for the duration of the regime. I guess he should be proud that he saved his own life and his family.

I was a bit confused about one thing. If the Khmer Rouge planned to adopt Year Zero from the French Revolution of 1720, where the entire French Monarchy was executed, which was only a few thousand. Why did they keep Sihanouk and his wife? Why did they kill all the professionals? Why did they allow the harsh living conditions where millions of people, including children, died? Why was I subject to such harsh manual labor when I was only nine years old?

Moreover, I was not alone in wanting to understand why ordinary people became killers. Thet Sambath, a young survivor who lost most of his family members, spent his adult life in Cambodia searching to interview the Khmer Rouge soldiers. He became a documentary filmmaker in Cambodia. For years, he worked to gain the trust of former Khmer Rouge soldiers so they would open up to him. He recorded their stories, capturing their confessions about what they did during that time. Some of the interviews were chilling to watch, especially when a few of the men showed no emotion as they described killing truckloads of Lon Nol's soldiers. They were among the units called the "smashing unit." It was the execution team.

They wanted to know how it was possible to kill thousands of soldiers without any resistance. The Khmer Rouge explained how they had to lie and divide them into small groups.

"We told them that they could meet Sihanouk." Instead, they were taken one truck at a time to be killed.

"What happened when they found out that they were going to die?" They pushed for an answer.

"Some of them cursed at us, others sobbed uncontrollably, and others fell to the ground helplessly," one Khmer Rouge soldier described.

It was a chilling testimony. Yet, it lacked human compassion and remorse. There was no emotion or guilt. How could they live with themselves after what they did? Their only justification was to kill or be killed.

"I had no choice." One of the former Khmer Rouge soldiers told Thet.

"I had to pretend that I had no relation when I spotted my uncle among the group to be executed. I hid to make sure that he did not recognize me." These were the admissions of one of the Khmer Rouge soldiers. It was difficult for me to watch all of Thet's interviews. I could only imagine the kind of characteristics of the soldiers who admitted no wrongdoing. I understood the authoritarian mentality of the following order. However, I also believe in humanity, where there had to be reasons to take such drastic action of killing without conscience. I am concerned about the children of such killers. Are they continuing to live by following orders even though they know it to be wrong? In the end, did we really learn anything from our actions or inactions? I am more afraid of the inability to question ethics.

At the same time, I believe that Sihanouk was as guilty as the rest of the Khmer Rouge leadership. If only the Khmer Rouge soldiers and supporters admitted that what they participated in was not the action of ordinary people. I wish that they would at least accept some responsibility and understand that what they did was wrong. For example, the Khmer Rouge's children who bullied me during the time I was all alone realized that what they did was wrong. They were children, and I was a child with no relatives nearby when they decided to push me off the riverbank. To me, it was intentional. They treated me as though I did not deserve to live. For that reason, I hope they learn what human kindness is all about.

In addition, Lon Nol was a much worse leader than Sihanouk. Under his administration, he lost to the Khmer Rouge. How was it possible? He had the backing of the U.S. He was a weak man to be exploited by the Americans. He had no strategy to secure a safe passage for his people. The Khmer Rouge called Lon Nol's government "traitors and corrupted." Were they wrong?

In my view, the leadership of Cambodia failed me and my brothers. I only hope that the spirits of millions of people who perished during the Khmer Rouge forgave the leaders who did nothing for others but themselves.

Geopolitical

Some scholars attributed the rise of the Khmer Rouge in Cambodia to the geopolitical maneuver of the United States. While I believed the exploitation of a weak leader to gain an advantage in the territories was unethical and unconstitutional. However, the Khmer Rouge leaders and their supporters were responsible for the crimes committed during that period. They incited hatred and resentment on the group of individuals who had grown the economy, modernized arts and culture, and connected with the outside world through learning English and French. The Khmer Rouge leaders used foreigners as scapegoats to their ill intention on the population. The Khmer Rouge leaders exploited the uneducated population to do their dirty work in getting rid of people they deemed as threats.

It was evident that America employed geopolitics when it entered the Vietnam War in 1965. America sought to persuade Sihanouk, then the head of state, to support efforts to prevent communist Vietnam from dominating Southeast Asia. However, Sihanouk refused by claiming neutrality. While Sihanouk was out of the country, America exploited the second in command, General Lon Nol. Lon Nol was a conservative. His government was the Khmer Republic. It was grossly negligent for the U.S. to support a person without leadership skills. He failed. America also failed. Kamm (1998) noted that America was looking for a clean exit from Vietnam and that Washington did not care about the internal turmoil of the country it exploited. In fact, Kamm (1998) added that Lon Nol received between $200,000 and $1 million of pocket money to end his days in the United States. Therefore, whatever happened to the people was not a concern of the United States.

While I pledged my allegiance to the United States of America—my home, sanctuary, and the democracy that I cherished, I shuddered at the lack of integrity and ethics on the part of American political leaders during the era of the Vietnam War. I was disappointed to hear that my family and I were not considered in the game of war. We were the casualties that were expected to be crippled physically, mentally, and emotionally after the outcome. That was only if we lived to tell our stories. Those families who had completely perished had no one to testify as to how long their ancestry dated back to the Angkor era. Their properties were up for grabs by the opportunists. No one even felt the pain of losses like I felt after witnessing such cruelty being done to children and adults.

Moreover, what appalled me was that the US provided safe passage for Lon Nol and his family to flee Cambodia on April 1, where millions of innocent people became victims of the Khmer Rouge regime.

Indeed, politics was vicious. In the eyes of many Cambodians, Henry Kissinger was to blame for his aggressive foreign policy. To him, Cambodia was just collateral damage. He did not recognize any link to the five hundred tons of bombs dispersed across the Cambodian countryside during the Vietnam War. The bomb caused thousands of casualties and displaced many others. The event led rural folks to believe in Western dominance. The event forced people into desperation. They believed that the Khmer Rouge would offer a better security than any administration aligning with the United States. The misplaced trust led to genocide.

Kissinger viewed the Khmer Rouge as a tragedy. It was Cambodians killing Cambodians. It had nothing to do with his policy. Therefore, he believed his conscience was clear. Never mind the fact that the U.S. dropped twice as many tons of bombs on rural Cambodia as on Japan in World War II (Chandler, 2008). Afterward, there was no accountability or humanitarian support for the people who were in harm's way.

The action left resentment and allowed the seeds of hatred to grow.

However, I like to believe that because of the aggressive foreign policy deployed during the Vietnam War, Congress felt a sense of moral obligation to pass the Refugee Act of 1980, which allowed the largest groups of refugees to enter the United States from Southeast Asia, the majority from Vietnam. Cambodian refugees, including myself, also benefit from this Act. Therefore, efforts had been made to mend the broken trust of the West.

Furthermore, the contributing factor to the rise of the Khmer Rouge lay heavily on the French. How was it possible that they bore no shame after exploiting Cambodia for nearly a century? The Khmer Rouge harbored its hatred because of how insensitive the French were. Ironically, the leaders of the Khmer Rouge got involved in communism by learning from the French while they were studying in France. In 1864, the French added Cambodia to the list of protectorates, which eventually became a colony (Kamm, 1998). To generate maximum benefit, the French imported skilled workers and civic servants from Vietnam and China to explore the fertile land and untapped resources such as rubber and silk. For centuries, the Khmer people were taught to only take enough from nature to survive and live a peaceful life without greed. Yet, the French introduced greed with the capital "C," masking the growth of the nation. Yet, those who benefited the most were the minority group that the French brought in to expand the rubber plantation, rice and silk factories, and more. Not only did the minority groups do well with homeownership and seeking native labor for blue-collar jobs and servants, but they also lacked the education or credentials to earn higher-paying positions. As a result, they were insulted for being poor and lazy. The lack of ambition due to what Theravada Buddhism taught about having no greed was viewed by the newcomers as being lazy.

The French did not implement significant measures to promote education for all Cambodians, thereby limiting opportunities for upward mobility within various levels of government and industry. The Khmer Rouge knew of the hardship and resentment of the rural Khmer people toward city dwellers and ethnic minorities in the country. They viewed ethnic minorities as taking their jobs away from them and the city dwellers as being traitors and corrupt for allowing others to take advantage of the country. Moreover, Cambodia never forgave Vietnam for invading and successfully took South Vietnam and today Saigon for their own land expansion. Not to mention, when Vietnam occupied Cambodia, it forced the native Khmer to adopt its culture and language, treating the Khmer people as "Barbarians." The hatred of Vietnamese ethnicities is still in the blood of many older-generation Cambodian adults today. It was not just the tale of "Tare Ong" that was told by many generations, but the fact that in the 1800s, when Vietnam conquered Cambodia, it attempted to transform Cambodia into Vietnam by outlawing the Cambodian language, culture, and belief. The trauma from such enforcement left resentment and hatred for many generations to deal with. The French policies favored the Vietnamese ethnic group over the Indigenous Khmer, leading to increased disparities and tensions between the two groups. Perhaps, this hatred translated to the willingness to kill not just ethnic minorities but the educators who were assumed to be corrupted.

Perhaps Um (2015) was right when she suggested that compound trauma from almost a century of colonized exploitation by the French and multiple invasions from neighboring countries led to the need for national revival. She concluded that the Khmer Rouge aimed to create a perfect state, but it lost sight of the human dimension.

I agreed with the author about compound trauma. Perhaps, in the centuries of being victims, they became perpetrators. The Khmer Rouge exploited the mental health of people to bring about their communist ideology in Cambodia. At the same time, I wondered about the loss of trust in the thousands of years of Buddha's teaching. Why did they abandon the values they were taught? What happened to the principle of not harming others? While I understand the fact that external forces played a role in the Khmer Rouge coming to power, I believe that we all had a choice to do good for others. If the majority of the population had some kind of education on humanity and civility, perhaps the treatment of ordinary fellow citizens would have been adopted. Perhaps the casualties of war were minimized. It was the lack of common sense to put people first that coerced people into believing that only violence could solve centuries of conflict.

Social Dysfunction

Bit (1991) confirmed that Cambodian society lost its sense of coherence and solidarity due to political differences and trauma. Bit might be corrected in his point of view. It led me to believe that if the French had taken into consideration the historical trauma imposed by centuries of war from its neighbors, the outcome of the Khmer Rouge would have been different. Instead, the French thought only of how to generate quick revenues for themselves by bringing Vietnamese civil servants to run the colonizing administration. As a result, many Vietnamese immigrants were better off than the elite Khmer people. With economic improvement and the wealth increase among ethnic minorities came discrimination and bias. Capitalism was great. However, it neglected the people who were taught to be modest, earn inner peace, and have rather than be excessive. No one took into consideration giving an opportunity to those who were left behind by democracy in name but not in service. It was no wonder the Khmer Rouge assumed that all city dwellers were corrupted, including children. Sometimes, I heard the adults describe the condition prior to the Khmer Rouge as "buyable." Mom said that to pass the school exam, one had to study day and night. However, if one were a rich kid, one did not need a passing grade to graduate. Money talked. Money bought morals and ethics. It led me to believe that democracy only works for some people. The gap between rich and poor was severe enough that people were willing to lose their dignity and pride.

What If

What if the French took into consideration historical trauma and understood why the Khmer people loathed Vietnam as a State and its people? Wasn't the French offered a protection agreement to save Cambodia from becoming obsolete? Would the French still employ Vietnamese to run the colonized administration rather than train the Cambodians themselves to do the job for their own nation? I guessed the outcome would be different if one considered others' feelings before thinking of how much and how fast I could benefit from this country. I was disappointed at how adults viewed world peace in the past.

Apparently, there was no what-if in the 1800s. The winner took it all, as always. The French needed instant revenue. They explored the fertile soil for production and rice production. They used Chinese investors to harvest the abundance of freshwater creatures. They exported Cambodian rice as the world's best crop. They did not just exploit land but the people as well. Meanwhile, the poor and uneducated were taught to be aggressive to survive. Moreover, it was outrageous to the Indigenous Khmer to see the new wealthy group as Vietnamese or Chinese immigrants.

Subsequently, resentment, hatred, and paranoia took their form.

I was confused about one thing about people in the past. Thailand and Vietnam occupied Cambodia during their invasions. Yet, the Cambodian people seemed to remain respectable and courteous toward the Thai people but loathed the Vietnamese. Perhaps the attempt to change Cambodian identity is what set off such hatred and resentment.

Chandler (2008) confirmed that during the early 1800s, when Vietnam controlled Cambodia, Emperor Minh Mang wished for Vietnamese Cambodians. Mang wanted Cambodians to eat, talk, behave, and be like the Vietnamese, so he sent groups of prisoners to be embedded among the Cambodian people in every sector of living (Chandler, 2008). He wished to indoctrinate them into the Vietnamese culture. Even Chandler was outraged that the Emperor of Vietnam sent prisoners instead of proper guides with diplomacy skills to convert Cambodians into Vietnamese. For me, it made sense to break the bad the Cambodian people. Since Angkor Wat was built, people were taught to be kind and compassion to live in harmony. As a result, people became too weak to defend themselves against invaders. Perhaps the emperor of Vietnam at the time thought that we might need to learn how to protect ourselves from within to release criminals in the country instead of the good ones.

Perhaps my aunt Dara was right. She believed the Khmer Rouge, who killed millions, were all double agents of Vietnam. They pretended to be Cambodians in order to wipe out the existence of the descendants from the Khmer Angkor period. It was always the wish of the Vietnam's Emperor to absorb all the Khmer land permanently. Aunt Dara's perspective was consistent with the views held by many Cambodian adults. They could not bring themselves to believe that the Khmer people were capable of being the perpetrators. Yet, all I saw was the Khmer people.

I often wondered about the deep hatred of the Vietnamese ethnic. Racism is carried even in the State and in this century. I understood what Mang did was undignified, yet as humans, we learned nothing from the past. I wanted to know if the Khmer people of the past carried their hatred in the form of nationally acceptable wording. For example,

"Som-Law-Ma-Jew-Yoon." The words meant Vietnamese sour soup. It could also mean soup made in Vietnamese. I also heard it was the soup inspired by Vietnamese cuisine. It depended on who I asked and what their bias level was about the Vietnamese people.

Or it could mean the same thing as the food named "French Fries." One thing I learned about our elders was that they were not shy about expressing their feelings. The decline of the Khmer Empire began in the 14th century. There was a time where Thailand occupied the city of Angkor Wat. Ankor Wat was the spirit and soul of the Khmer people. They persisted and regained control of the province, which they subsequently named Siem Reap. It meant "Siem Kneel." Thailand used to be called Siam. Siam or the Khmer called it "Siem," which meant "Thief" in the Thai language. Perhaps they changed the name from "Siam" to "Thai" and added "Land" to Thailand to rebrand themselves away from the origin of untrustworthy. The Cambodians' prior generations had some resentment toward Thailand when they occupied Angkor Wat. Yet, the similarity in culture, language, religion, and food attracted the Cambodian people to remain courteous toward the Thai people.

Moreover, as the population became diverse, so did the discrimination. Adding to political unrest due to inequality and unjust for the poor, society "was corrupted," as the Khmer Rouge believed.

How was it possible for any responsible adult to do nothing about it? If the French failed to care enough about the people who did not want to commercialize every farm as the French insisted, so that they could produce more rice and vegetables to be sold outside, no one in the leadership role provided education for sustainability. Instead, the social function created layers of restriction and enforced high taxes for the individual farmers to exist as they had been for centuries.

On top of everything, the social interaction among different groups of people created tensions to co-exist. While the generation of wealthy Khmer people looked down on the new money like Chinese and Vietnamese immigrants, the new immigrants discriminated against the poor Khmer people. For example, I heard from the Chinese Cambodian adults who told me how the Khmer children bullied her.

"Go back to China" was a common insulting phrase, while other Chinese Cambodians viewed the Khmer people as being lazy and uncivilized. They even encouraged their children not to marry the Indigenous Khmer but only Chinese Cambodians because they would be more ambitious and educated.

In addition, societal preference and perception created division among groups. The poor people were more in despair because they had no opportunity for upward mobility. They had no formal education. If they could read, they learned from each other or at the Buddhist Temples. To make matters worse, those parents with daughters told their daughters to marry Chinese Cambodian men because they tended to be more ambitious and stable economically, whereas the Khmer men tended to lack ambition, were uneducated, and had no greed. At the same time, I have heard from the Chinese Cambodian family not to marry a Khmer woman because she did not value wealth and kept the family prosperous in terms of monetary terms.

This kind of message had gone on for years. I wondered when the Khmer Rouge ordered the execution of ethnic minorities such as Chinese, Vietnamese, and Cham (Muslim) because they blamed such rhetoric existed. Being identified as Chinese, Vietnamese, or Cham was not enough for the Khmer Rouge. Anyone who had a light skin tone was also a target of elimination. Was hatred the motivation? My poor father had light skin because he worked indoors all his life. I wanted to know my ancestry, so I took a DNA test. Yes, I was six percent Vietnamese. Perhaps the Khmer Rouge already thought that people who were born in the city were somewhat compromised by having multi-ethnicity.

Indeed, the Khmer Rouge sought to purify Cambodians, as suggested by Um (2015). They were willing to commit genocide just to return to what it was. They killed ethnic minorities such as the Vietnamese and Chinese out of despair they felt. They killed monks because religion was used for centuries to justify inequity in society. They killed educated individuals because they were afraid of the uprising. They killed art, culture, and entertainers because they wanted people to focus on productivity. There was no democracy, no freedom, no rights, and no basic dignity.

Moreover, the Khmer Rouge sought to abandon any words that the city dwellers adopted. I was confused when I was told not to use "corrupted" words such as "Pa" and "Mak." Since I was born, I only knew the words Pa and Mak. What was so wrong with it? Indeed, the word "Pa" was not a Khmer word. It was a Chinese word. It meant "Dad." The word "Mak" had its origin from China, from the word "Ma," which means "Mom." Was losing the Khmer language enough for the Khmer Rouge to kill?

The Khmer Rouge forced me to call my parents "Pok" (dad) and "Mare" (mom), as the country folks would call their parents. They were the Khmer words. At first, I thought about the pettiness of its leader, Saloth Sar. However, I understood his fear of losing the Khmer language. Perhaps he used this fear to gain the support of the rural populations by telling them the Khmer identity would be replaced with Chinese and Vietnamese soon enough. Perhaps the fear of extinction forced people to turn to the dark side.

Religion:

I did not expect that the Khmer Rouge would abandon thousands of years of religion, Buddhism. How did the Khmer Rouge think that Buddhist monks were also corrupted? They killed the monks with higher positions and forced many to disrobe, like Mak Yay's nephew, Soveoun Ven, under their control. Why did they hate the religion that they were brought up to believe in? Could religion be used to exploit and oppress people as well? Certainly, I knew of it to be. For instance, there was no program to assist the poor, yet those who were in charge claimed that it was karma to be born poor, as though we had a choice to whom we were born into. This kind of reasoning was a way to suppress people from learning about human rights. That we all deserve to live with dignity, regardless of what situation we were born into. Using karma and fate to tell people that they did not deserve to be equal was despicable. Walker (2022) reminded us that religion is a perfect hiding place for a false self-image. What price must we pay to conceal our own bias under the false pretense of religion?

We were supposed to be better human beings because we chose to believe in something besides ourselves. Growing up, monks were the symbol of Buddhism. At every event, I would have to bow and *som-past* (putting both palms together) in acknowledgment and respect. Monks represented

Buddha at weddings, funerals, holidays, and even regular spiritual gatherings. Buddhism was essential to everyday living for many Cambodians. The branch of Buddhism that many Cambodians practiced was called "Theravada Buddhism." It meant the "teaching of the elders." I could only assume that our faith influences our generations of respecting our parents and authority figures. However, when our parents and authority figures made decisions based on their own needs, the younger generations had few options to change. If one went against the wishes of the elders, one was viewed as "Kone Ott Poojch" (a kid with no ancestry).

Mak Yay was raised with Buddha's principles. She did not smoke, drink alcohol, lie, cheat, steal, be unfaithful, nor do harm to others. When she was healthy, she would get up each morning at four am to chant for at least forty-five minutes. I was in the State in 1983. I was to repeat the verse after her. She began her day with the clearing of her mind. It was supposed to be good for the soul, she said.

I was half asleep each morning as I tried sitting behind her with my left leg folded inside and my right leg folded outside on the floor. I would never reach enlightenment because I did not take chanting seriously. Besides, most of the words were Sanskrit, and I did not understand the meaning. What was so amazing about my grandma was that she was illiterate, not by choice, but by circumstances, yet she remembered each word from how the monks preached. Mak Yay never lost her faith when she waited for us to get out of the Khmer Rouge. She waited eight years to be reunited with her other five children. It broke her heart to find out that she lost three grandsons, my brothers, and her favorite son-in-law, my father. Nevertheless, she embraced us as we began our lives over again in Southern California. Mak Yay did believe that her good deeds paid off.

On the other hand, Mom used religion to justify her sorrow of losing three sons. Mom was raised to believe that even killing animals was wrong. But during the Khmer Rouge, when we were starving, Dad found three toads in a rice field. He was so happy, and my three brothers and I were excited; we finally had something with protein to eat. Even though it went against Mom's beliefs, she had no choice but to cook the toads for us. She had no choice. She was desperate to ensure our well-beings. We were thrilled to allow our young digestive system something to work on. At the same time, Mom believed that because she sinned, she deserved to lose three sons. In reality, it was the Khmer Rouge that killed my brothers. They enforced cruelty even for children to survive.

As an educated woman, I was disappointed in my mother. How could she compare the lives of her sons to the lives of the toads? At the same time, I accepted her belief that it meant easing the pain of loss for her.

Culture:

I was taught to be respectful to elders, titles, and ranking within family members at a young age. I was told to listen to my parents and teachers. I was told to use proper words to call family members. However, I remember having challenged my Mom on the social order of name-calling. For example, Mak Yay was still having a kid when Mom was having a kid. My youngest uncle was a year younger than I was.

I was told to call him "Lok Mear" (Uncle Sir). I protested, thinking that I was a year older; didn't I have more privilege?

"He is your uncle. Therefore, he has status." Mom explained. Apparently, status was more important than age. We referred to people with titles and positions. It explained the culture of obedience. At the same time, the class system gave honorific distinctions.

However, during the Khmer Rouge, we were told to change our wording if we wanted to live. Mak Yay learned class etiquette from her great-great-grandparents' in-laws once she settled in the city upon marriage at eighteen. I learned that there were words to address different class groups, such as the royal, noble, monk, upper, and middle. For example, the word "eat" was enforced during the Khmer Rouge as "ហូប" (pronounce hope). The Khmer Rouge adopted the most commonly used word by rural populations. The word "ហូប" supposed to symbolize equality. Perhaps, the Khmer Rouge used the word to ensure the trust by the rural population.

I became familiar with the word "ញុាំ" (jmum) during my childhood. It also meant to eat. The word is used among children in the city. If I were to ask my parents or grandparents to eat dinner, I would use the word "Peik Sar." The royal used the word "Souv." The monk used "Chun."

Social classes divided people. While the idea of achieving equal treatment for every citizen was admirable, the Khmer Rouge went overboard to rid people simply because of their previous class. The Khmer Rouge used force to conduct social changes rather than allowing them to change on their own. However, the Khmer Rouge's policy of allowing the rural people the privilege of being a leader without basic education did not recreate equal treatment for every citizen either.

I understand that the Khmer Rouge wanted to create an equal society by eliminating the ranking system using words to distinguish classes; what I did not understand was the cruelty and brutality being done to city dwellers. I wanted to know who was in charge of Pursat, the notorious province for inflicting so much pain on others. Besides the top Khmer

Rouge leaders who were brought to justice, would the lower-level Khmer Rouge leaders ever have realized that what they did to their own people was wrong? The silence of those involved in the deaths of millions was particularly troubling to me. It was the base people who treated me and my brothers as though we did not deserve to live that still haunted me because no one admitted having committed such crimes against humanity.

Perhaps James Waller, the author of "Becoming Evil: How Ordinary People Commit Genocide and Mass Killing," said it best. "The conditions under which many of us could be transformed into killing machines." His theory supported the analysis of Katharya Um, the author of "From the Land of Shadows: War, Revolution, and the Making of the Cambodia Diaspora." Um suggested that the compounded trauma from colonization, multiple invasions, and the betrayal of the government led to the Khmer Rouge. Did the conditions justify changing ordinary people into perpetrators? Perhaps society should take more of a social responsibility to agree that what would affect one group could eventually affect others.

I remembered a happy childhood with my family prior to the Khmer Rouge. Was it because my parents sheltered me from what was going on out there in society? I got to see the last facial expression of my father and paternal grandfather. I saw regret and disappointment on their faces. They were more afraid for us than for themselves. Could it be the realization that they should have done better to contribute to society as a whole? Could it be that the idea of respecting authority figures led them to stay away from politics? There was a sense of sadness and disbelief. My father was a devoted, kind, and responsible person. Perhaps he thought it was enough to be a member of society. Yet, he did look as though he had failed me and my brother in that last moment before he returned to death. The price for good people who did nothing to change the culture and society in which they raised their children was enormous. We should learn from the past.

Chapter Seven
Prolonged Grief

"It has been said that time heals all wounds. I don't agree. The wounds remain. In time, the mind, protecting its sanity, covers it with scar tissue, and the pain lessens. But it is never gone."

– Rose Kennedy

Time

Rose Kennedy was right. Time does not automatically heal internal wounds. I was waiting for time to heal my wound for over forty years. I was hoping for time to wipe away the sad memories from my childhood during the Khmer Rouge regime in Cambodia between 1975 and 1979. I was waiting for time to give back the innocent thought of goodness in every human being. Yet, time does not automatically take away my pain of losses. It did not erase the bad images from my memories. In my heart, I still feel the wound. My internal wound has no expiration date.

When the thought of the Khmer Rouge era came to mind, I shivered in disbelief. It was an unimaginable outrage. It was like national violence against certain groups of people: military opposition, political opposition, the established class with long-term wealth passing down for generations, the educated class, and the white-collar professionals such as my parents. Why were they the target of the revolution, just because they could motivate people to work? Retired law enforcement personnel, like my grandfathers, were not viewed fondly by the new society. What did they do wrong during their jobs fifty years earlier? Entertainers such as the great musicians in the country, what did they do wrong to eliminate them as well? As far as I could tell, their music brought such joy to countless individuals. What about the monks? What did they do wrong but preach kindness and compassion? Why persecute them? It was unreal to look back at the history of an attempt to wipe out a society that was progressing, leaving marginalized people to want a different society for existence. It was close to the totalitarian society that Margaret Atwood imagined in her book The Handmaid's Tale.

Therefore, time does not erase my memories from my childhood. Time has allowed me to prolong my grief.

Denial

I was protecting my sanity when I denied my past. It was my way of coping by pretending that I had a normal childhood.

In high school, I made friends from diverse backgrounds. I enjoyed learning about their challenges growing up. It was nothing compared to me, and yet I believe that I was as normal as they were. When it was my turn to share my background, I only spoke of my experience of being a refugee, but nothing about my losses and suffering during the Khmer Rouge regime. I avoided recalling memories that would make me cry.

In my twenties, I denied myself an identity. I never volunteered to share with people where I came from unless I was specifically asked. When people I came across, whether at school or work, assumed that I was Filipina or Vietnamese, I just let them think so.

Somehow, I believed it was better to be an immigrant than a refugee. I was ashamed of myself. I did not want other people my age to know about my horrible childhood during the Khmer Rouge for almost four years.

I was not aware that denial was a form of trauma. I knew it was prolonged grief. There was no real end to how I felt inside. As long as I stayed busy, I didn't have the time or energy to reflect on the past. I threw myself into tasks, burying the emotions beneath a packed schedule. Balancing a full-time job while attending school full-time was difficult but manageable. It was not easy, but eventually, I completed each step as I progressed in education. I earned an Associate of Science degree from El Camino College, a Bachelor of Arts from National University, and a master's degree in human resources from Chapman University.

In addition, I got to live an independent life just like many American young women I knew. It was not simple for a Cambodian culture to allow a daughter to move out and live on her own before marriage, even though I could afford to live on my own. However, Mom was not a simple woman. She was educated. She knew the potential of being free to make decisions. Besides, I made a compelling case for safety and saving time by not commuting long distances at night. Mom agreed. However, Mom faced scrutiny from relatives and friends for breaking the norm. It was unheard of to allow the only surviving daughter to go off on her own without the eyes and ears of family members to watch over her. The unforeseeable force would not be kind to me. They were acting on their own fears when they reminded Mom of the evils out there in the world. Thank God that Mom did not allow their negative imagination to prevent her from supporting my wishes. Moreover, I was never irresponsible in my behavior, which caused her to worry.

In this respect, I was lucky to have a Mom like my mom. For the first time, I felt liberated. I began to realize that I could make my own decision. I could sleep whenever I wanted to. I could drive along the coast without being afraid that I would cross the perimeter of the campsite. I was able to feel normal for the first time. I was able to sleep soundly without being worried that I would be taken in the night, as the disappearance of many children in the camp. I saw the possibility in life.

Unresolved Grief

How can we ever come to terms with our trauma when justice did not prevail? There was an attempt to find justice for the million victims who perished. The UN-backed Khmer Rouge tribunal that finally ended in 2022 attempted to satisfy the justice system. The result of the sixteen-year effort led to three convictions of former Khmer Rouge leaders. Unfortunately, Pol Pot, brother number one, leader of the Khmer Rouge, a.k.a Saloth Sar, died in 1998. He never stood trial for crimes against humanity. In addition, Prince Norodom Sihanouk was never brought to trial for his involvement with the Khmer Rouge. How would the families of the victims find closure when justice is seen through different lenses of glasses? How could victims forgive when perpetrators failed to understand that what they did was not ethical and moral?

Unresolved grief persisted because closure and reconciliation had not been achieved. In the meantime, the adults who went through the Khmer Rouge, the adults who escaped the Khmer Rouge, and the adults who went through the Khmer Rouge without being persecuted because they did not belong to the targeted groups, continued to have different points of view of what went wrong. Some adults saw no fault in the Khmer Rouge and blamed external forces for their conduct. Some adults accepted the unjust world altogether, resigning from learning the facts that might explain the cause and consequence of the events that took place in 1975 in Cambodia.

The people and community continued to struggle to find closure, whether individually or in groups, through activities to share the common ground. What remained true was that we needed each other to exist. We came together to celebrate and to share our pride in having such great arts and culture. Yet deep down, we feared each other, especially when there was conflict due to differences of opinion. For this reason, unresolved grief remained within us.

Many older adults who faced difficulty in the homeland and lacked the knowledge to adapt to the new environment found themselves physically debilitated. Some adults, like Mom's cousin, who survived the Khmer Rouge, were monks, a target group, and failed to value how important their lives were. He passed away due to asthma, a disease that could be remedied. He always looked out for others but not himself. He saved all his earnings for his son but neglected his own health due to the high cost of asthma medication. If he thought that after what he had been through, life was more precious to him, he would live for his son and see the beautiful world unfold in the twenty-first century. Yet, trauma consumed him. Maybe he felt too overwhelmed to keep going after his experiences. Instead of seeking help to relieve the pressure of witnessing the lowest point in humanity, he just wanted to rest in peace. Indeed, he did. Leaving his son, wife, and those who admired him to mourn a great man. I wished that I could slow down the death rate among survivors. I wished that I could help them realize how important it was for them to appreciate the lives that they had, knowing what they knew. For those Survivors who lived within walking distance of community organizations, they found some emotional and mental support through cultural activities. However, most older adults living far away from walking distance of the community found it lonesome to be all alone while their children were at work or at school. As a result, learning to resolve one's own grief was impossible to achieve. However, the topic of genocide remained sensitive, and some refused to acknowledge that it was history.

The complexity of the inability to recognize and support the efforts of closure was that the Cambodian community had many different groups. For some survivors who did not face great persecution felt somehow ashamed that they were lucky to be in a better province and were not in the target groups. For some privileged Cambodians who got a chance to escape prior to 1975 would have different types of political opinions, and the degree of prideful would never admit how cruel the Cambodian people were to each other during the Khmer Rouge regime. It was guilt, shame, and denial that kept them from coming to terms with historical trauma.

While time did not heal my wounds from the past, time protected my sanity by keeping me preoccupied with self-reflection. I used time to adjust to the new environment as I settled in my new country, America, as a refugee. I started from the bottom by learning the country's primary language, English. I had to learn how to think independently when I was taught to take orders and to work hard. I was taught not to have any opinion, whether right or wrong; I was supposed to keep them to myself. I never raised my hand in class. When I was called upon, I was timid to answer any question. I watched and learned how other teenagers gave their opinions freely. I was not taught to be as free as they were. Before the Khmer Rouge, I was taught to be respectful to adults regardless of what they said. During the Khmer Rouge, I was taught to shut up and do the work or else. I was still adjusting to life outside of a barbed-wire fence in the refugee camp or under the supervision of the children's camp during the Khmer Rouge regime. I had to learn how to live outside the perimeter.

One thing I knew how to do well was working. The Khmer Rouge had trained me to work since I was just nine years old. The Khmer Rouge had me carry a huge bundle of rice string freshly cut by the adults onto the dry area by the walkway. At a children's camp, I was plowing the field for gardening. Sometimes, the only break I got was dinner and night. Each day was filled with assigned duties, and there was no time left for me to think about my family and the condition I was living in.

When we came to the State, like many other Cambodian refugees, Mom and her family tried their luck in the donut store. It was a manual-intensive kind of work. My job after work was to clean trays, pots, and pans. I mopped the floor. I learned the name of each donut so that I could serve the customers correctly. It was practicing English for me. Running the donut store was not in the DNA of my family. The business was not successful partly due to the location, and we eventually quit, and each of us focused on education and obtaining jobs outside of small businesses.

However, learning to speak English fluently took away most of my time. I often encountered laughter and bias because of an imperfect accent. Regardless of the insensitivity I encountered, I never allowed the biased behaviors of others to interfere with my effort to assimilate into my new society.

There was no doubt that I would succeed in life due to hard work, determination, and drive. The fact that I had never stopped learning contributed to my personal and professional growth. However, no matter how much I grew personally and professionally, in my heart, I felt hollow due to the atrocity. I was driven to seek more significant achievements in my career.

Knowing what I know now, I understand my feelings of guilt for being alive. Reflecting on the past forty years, I feel like I lived four lives. I was trying to embody the characteristics of my youngest brother, Phirum, who was only six years old when he died during the Khmer Rouge regime. His kindness and honesty stayed with me. His heart was pure, and his love was real and unconditional. I saw how deeply he loved our dog. When the dog was shot as we were leaving our home, Phirum was heartbroken and completely lost. At the same time, I was living with my second brother, Varen, who was nine at the time. He was competent, faithful, and smart. I tried so hard to be like him. I often wondered what he could accomplish in life if he had a chance to live. I worked so hard to fulfill every commitment I had made because that was just how Varen operated. When he set a goal, he would accomplish it regardless of difficulty. He was a year younger than I was; he could do as much work as I did during the Khmer Rouge. Finally, my brother Baron, who was eight years old when he died. Mom said he made it to January of 1977. He was brave, courageous, and helpful to others. He was my hero. He saved me multiple times. He protected me from being persecuted just because I was a kid who was born in the city. He kept me mobile by sharing extra protein to include edible insects. He was by my side until the day he died. As for me, the only time I felt that I lived for myself was when I became a mother. It was pure joy.

As I reflected on the saddest event from my childhood, I realized that I am not alone. The ugly stain in my heart and mind was shared by millions of Cambodian refugees scattered around the world. Although their experience might be different than mine, I hope that they will find a way to forgive the past and learn from it.

I learned from my past as I went back to school. At first, the pursuit of a higher education was to restore the educational values that were lost because of the Khmer Rouge. Since the Khmer Rouge targeted educators and professional individuals who kept the economy moving, the fears of persecution remained in many survivors that they felt encouraged their second generation to pursue higher education. As a result, the shortage of leaders and the slow progress within communities suffered.

Working in the Cambodian community in Long Beach, California, I saw firsthand the impact of historical trauma on survivors and their families. It was obvious that basic necessity was the priority. While small businesses contributed a great deal to the economy, education was no longer a priority. They failed to see education as an investment for upward mobility. How could they? When they saw what the Khmer Rouge did to the educated population. They still believed ignorance was bliss. The American Community Survey released data indicating that Cambodian Americans have the lowest rate of higher educational attainment. As a result, there is a shortage of representation and leaders within community sectors. There is a shortage of teachers, nurses, caregivers, and other professionals in many areas within the community. In addition, the high percentage of community members living below the federal poverty line was obvious.

I wanted to know whether trauma played a role in many survivors who witnessed the killing of educators or someone with the ability to read and write. Or perhaps our educational system failed to inspire younger generations to pursue higher education.

I also sought the opportunity to find closure. Unconsciously, I realized that I had watched many shows on TV, and it was all about solving and investigating murders. Some of my favorite shows were NCIS, Forensic Files, and FBI. I concluded that I, too, wanted to solve the discomfort in my heart. I wanted to understand why kind and gentle people hated each other so much that they resorted to inflicting suffering on one another, especially on children. By knowing the reasons, I hope to achieve peace of mind. I did not want to continue having such mistrust and resentment toward my own people because of what I saw they did to each other during the Khmer Rouge.

While many survivors and some historians blamed the insurrection of the Khmer Rouge regime on external factors, I blamed the rise of the Khmer Rouge on internal ones. Yes, outside forces may have provided the weapons, but it was the internal anger and pain that pulled the trigger. It felt like revenge for centuries of injustice and built-up emotions. The Khmer Rouge leaders let that anger explode, and it was taken out on by innocent people. For this reason, the party responsible should be all the leaders, including Prince Norodom Sihanouk, who supported the Khmer Rouge.

Ironically, my mom's generation did not see the falsehood of Sihanouk. She was born to respect authorities with no questions asked. She would always view him as the father of the country. At the same time, my aunt blamed the killing of millions of Cambodians on Vietnam, not the Khmer Rouge.

It was her theory that Vietnam would do anything to take Cambodia. They tried multiple times during the early years of invasions. In order to take the country, they had to kill the people. My aunt Dara had her own way of deflecting guilt onto another ethnicity. It was the only way that she could accept that ordinary Khmer people could become killers without trying to understand the conditions that led them to behave viciously.

"It was Vietnam's dream to own Cambodia," she said.

It had been centuries since Vietnam invaded Cambodia. Yet, in the minds of older-generation Cambodians, Vietnam- ese remained the "historic enemy." The Khmer Rouge targeted the killing of ethnic minorities such as Vietnamese, Chinese, and Chams in the country. In the minds of survivors, why didn't they hate Japanese or Thai people for many centuries as well? Those countries did invade Cambo- dia as well. What was it about the French? They did worse than any other dictator; why didn't many Khmer adults express their hatred for them?

The love-hate relationship between the Vietnamese and Cambodians had to stop. If they became more educated, they would know that it was political actions of the time, and it was nothing personal about the people themselves. There should be no more grudges and resentment toward the neighboring country. One thing I was confused about was that if the Vietnamese were the "historic enemies" of Cambodia, how come no one protested when the French imported a large group to work throughout their colonization administration? Did the French care about Cambodia? Did it help Cambodia to build a good relationship with Vietnam?

Now, I understand why many people stopped identifying themselves as having Vietnamese descent. They met with great discrimination. For example, my paternal grandmother was fluent in Vietnamese. When I asked if she had Vietnamese ancestry, no one in her family would admit anything. When I asked Mom, she would say.

"Well, she grew up in a town surrounded by Vietnamese immigrants, so she learned to speak Vietnamese well." There was no logical explanation except to hide one's identity to avoid discrimination based on race.

When I challenged my aunt about blaming the killing during the Khmer Rouge on the Vietnamese, I asked her, "How? I only saw the rural Khmer people commit violent acts against Khmer people."

"They brainwashed the Khmer people to kill each other so they could take over the country." It was her explanation.

I decided to shut down the conversation before I triggered any trauma. She was protecting her sanity by believing the "historic enemy" that was told to her decades ago. My aunt is a good and kind person. However, her judgment had been compromised due to her experience.

I wondered if the Khmer Rouge had not happened, would I have grown up believing that the "Vietnamese" were bad people? If that was the case, I, too, had relatives who were of Vietnamese descent on my father's side of the ancestry in high-ranking military personnel. He and his family got to come to the United States via military ships fleeing from the Khmer Rouge. He and his family were regarded highly. Was it because he was educated and had a high position? Did the people of the past only discriminate against the low-ranking Vietnamese the same as the Chinese immigrants? The more I tried to understand the people of the past, I began to doubt the innocence of my family.

If they lived in a culture and society that allowed others to dehumanize certain groups of people, they were also the culprits of this act of violence against their loved ones. To this observation, as a child who went through the ordeal, I blamed the adults for not shaping an environment that is conducive to growth through love, positivity, equality, justice, and liberty for all.

I understand that a civilized society does not just one day commit such horrific crimes against one another. The breeding of such violence happened way before the conflict in Southeast Asia.

As leadership declined and the Khmer empire failed, the French took the opportunity to be the "protector" of Cambodia. At the same time, the French saw the potential for revenues. To maximize productivity and increase revenue, the French brought instant investors from China to handle the growing economy and skillful Vietnamese immigrants to manage the administrative functions of a colonizing government.

Without cultivating the Khmer people to engage in progress, social tensions and division were inevitable. The Khmer people found themselves excluded from decision-making in education, economics, society, and politics. Social norms degraded Khmer men.

I grew up hearing about the achievements of Chinese Cambodian men in education and business. According to the Khmer elders they would be an ideal husband. Somehow, it was common perception among the elders in the community. Having grown up and received my education within mainstream American society, my perspectives have diverged from those of the adults in my community.

"A Chinese Cambodian man is better at saving." I often heard from the adults. The assumption that Chinese Cambodian men were more ambitious than Khmer men was absurd. Yet, people believed it was true. I wondered who pushed such narratives. I had some friends who had the same view and did as tell by their parents. I also heard the Khmer families would use a phrase to remind their children about saving by saying, "Chinese immigrants travel to Cambodia with just a leg of pickle crab." The phrase implied being stingy. To me, it symbolized enduring hardship while seeking growth across the ocean.

Conversely, I had my own bias from my experiences during the Khmer Rouge. It was the first time community eating in which the bigger Chinese Cambodian kids grabbed the food for themselves while my brothers and other young children looked on in disgust. Since then, I've never had a positive view of this group of people. I didn't like how selfish they were and how they didn't consider others. They had no manners. I saw no sense of pride or goodness in them. It felt like they were taught to put themselves first, without any feeling of guilt or regret. I was even upset at my parents for not teaching us to be ruthless like them. I was not prepared to interact with other children with no consideration for others. Perhaps the Khmer Rouge thought it was the best way to get rid of weak individuals by having us fight among each other.

Twenty-four years later, I married a Chinese Cambodian refugee who survived the Khmer Rouge in a less affected province than mine. Somehow, I thought of myself as a hypocrite for going against my own beliefs. Perhaps I was trying to test the theory of ambition and the love of money from the group that I despised in attitude and behaviors of "me first" without any consideration of others. Or perhaps the timing was right, and the opposite attracted. I temporarily forgot about the old grudge I had during the Khmer Rouge. Or it was possible that my biological clock was ringing, and I could not pass up the opportunity. His proficiency in working with elderly individuals, including my mother, greatly impressed me.

There was a Khmer proverb that said, "SaOpp Jom Pok Ler." In English, it would be referred to as "Never say Never."

I used to justify the union of my relationship as the "Yin" and "Yang." As for the stereotype of "ambition and saving," there was some truth to it. Besides spending on essentials and necessities, he did not like to waste any money. Since we got married, I have never received flowers from him. However, I used to obtain practical items. If I feel the need to refresh myself with the aroma of flowers, I just buy them to decorate the home and to enjoy the scenery.

When our sons were younger, they loved Christmas lights. Whenever they saw the neighbors put up the holiday lights, they would insist that we do the same. However, we would meet with resistance from Dad.

"No, it's a waste."

"But Dad! It's a beautiful waste." My younger son pleads.

Every year, we debated whether putting up the Christmas lights was a waste of energy and money versus joining the neighborhood in solidarity over a bright light. Of course, Dad was always outnumbered. I maintained the balance between practical and imaginable.

Stereotypes are used to divide people. I believe the society that led up to the Khmer Rouge was severely broken. The biased rhetoric between classes, races, religion, and justice. Messages were used to put down one group and to lift the other group. Messages had consequences.

How was it possible that no one stopped such rhetoric from spreading? Did the Khmer Rouge resend such messages when they committed genocide on ethnic minorities such as the Chinese, Vietnamese, and Chams?

I could not help but try to understand what justified the crime. What happened to the Khmer population that embodied kindness and compassion? For almost a century under French colonization, society and culture became blind to the injustice and inequity within the country. Was it despair and resentment that turned into hatred? Was it almost one hundred years of tolerance and being demeaned by the economic prosperity classes that got the Khmer Rouge to seek such drastic measures? Was it greed by the country's monarch who banned any opposition party from attempting to seek better lives for others? The Khmer Rouge called themselves Democratic Kampuchea.

It certainly seemed to be a perfect storm that swept away Cambodia's existence. The Khmer Rouge took advantage at the right moment to strike when tensions were high in the Southeast Asia peninsula. The plan of eliminating toxins in the country almost worked, except the price was too great.

The Khmer Rouge's leadership was not stable to begin with. For example, Pol Pot. He knew that what he was about to instigate was harmful. Why else did he choose the pseudonym Pol Pot? He was born as Saloth Sar. If his intention was purely for the greater good of the country, he would take pride in being who he was. When the Khmer Rouge banned Buddhist monks and all religions, was it because what Saloth Sar was about to do went against the Buddhist belief of "do the right thing"? Was it to spare his conscience if he was to still believe that all humans were born good? Or did he change his name to spare his family from being persecuted for what he did? No, he did it because he was ashamed of himself. In the process, he chose someone else's surname to be a bad person.

For years, I hated my surname, Pol. I was afraid that people would mistake me for Pol Pot's relative. Indeed, I was asked whether I was related to him. Even if some people might know that Pol Pot was his alias, they could not help assuming I was related to that monster. More importantly, I despised Saloth Sar for what he did to children like me during the Khmer Rouge. I wondered what my father and paternal grandfather would think of Saloth Sar using their surname to commit crimes against humanity. Would they forgive Saloth Sar for what he did? I would not. I would not forgive the leadership of the Khmer Rouge. What they did to children was unforgivable.

Nevertheless, I forgave the Khmer Rouge supporters. They too were victims of conspiracy theories. They believed that what they did was preserving the country's identity. They were misled by the Khmer Rouge leadership. Granted, they wanted the society to be fair. They wanted the same treatment, opportunity, and engagement just like people in the city with great influence. They did not want to be labelled as unmotivated and less ambitious just because they enjoyed the carefree living in the countryside. Perhaps, their resentment of city folks allowed them to trust the Khmer Rouge leaders blindly.

After the Khmer Rouge, many rural town folks returned to their villages, back to living a simple life, where some folks chose to leave the country, fearing retribution if they stayed.

Despite the cruelty and the senseless killings, there was remorse or kindness shown toward me and Mom as well. While Mom did not contribute to our survival to Mett Nang and Srey, I did.

Without Srey, I would not be here. She chose to save me. She intervened at a crucial moment when the welfare of children was often overlooked. My life was of no significance. Mom and I should be grateful to Mett Nang and Srey.

It has been fifty years. I do not know whether Mett Nang and Srey still existed. I would want to know why they were compelled to save me. Perhaps, they did it as good deed. Or perhaps, they realized what they had supported was unjust. It could be that they felt sorry for Mom. They could not stand by to see Mom lost everything. After all, Mom proved to her that she could perform any task with limited nutrition and attempted to break her soul by separating her family unit, making her suffer as she lost her son one by one. It took the camp leader months to tell Mom that her husband had died. What justification is to assume that all city dwellers were corrupt and did not deserve to live, even children? How could anyone believe blindly without using moral judgment? Then again, we should beware of a culture that gave absolute power to one person and the quest for absolute obedience.

As a young survivor, I feel a sense of obligation to do more. Simon Wiesenthal, a Holocaust survivor and the founder of the Museum of Tolerance, once said, "Survival is a privilege which entails obligations. I am forever asking myself what I can do for those who have not survived."

First, I believe that we all should take social responsibility for what messages we put out there. Because what we said as the norm could have such consequences in the future. I would continue to do something more than nothing in order to help shape the society that I want to live in with liberty and justice for all.

I am fortunate to learn from my past. It has helped me to inform my future and to be mindful about living with historical trauma. I live my life with the purpose of knowing how important life is. I used my experience to encourage myself to do better in the world because I realized that my actions or existence will have an impact on future generations.

By being aware of my past, I live every day in honor of my father and brothers. Previously, I felt I was living for my three brothers due to survivor guilt. Somehow, I felt sorry for being the only one to live where they did not. Therefore, I attempted to live my life for them in terms of accomplishment and ambition without thinking about what I really wanted for myself. I felt obligated to live on behalf of their young lives that were cut short due to preventable war if each of us looked out for others. It did not cause us much to be empathetic, kind-hearted, make no judgment, and more importantly, keep an open mind.

Otherwise, my brothers, father, grandparents, and millions of others would have an equal opportunity to live their lives. At the same time, survivors like me almost led my own lives to an early grave because of the historical trauma of feeling guilty to live because of mourning for those who did not get a chance to live.

Fortunately, it was not too late for me to realize that instead of trying to live my life for those I had lost, I should live my life in honor of theirs. A life with purpose, kindness, compassion, pride, integrity, good health, and good spirits by simply being thoughtful to family, friends, neighbors, communities, and country.

More importantly, taking the time to restore a sense of self as a human was important for me to see clearly what I wanted my life to be. I had seen too much of life without restoring what it was like to be treated humanely, where the dehumanized experience taught us to be defensive because we had been treated wrongly.

It was tiresome to live in self-defense mode for the rest of our lives. We had to slow down and allow ourselves to feel at ease in the environment that we were living in.

I have learned to enjoy the simplest things in life, like grocery shopping. I wondered about the aisles of diverse cultures in food and wished that I could cook them all. It was my way of telling myself that I was alive and that I would take in every moment I had.

Subconsciously, I went back to school to earn a doctoral degree in educational leadership to restore the value of education that was dehumanized during the Khmer Rouge. The revolution that targeted educators was the most cowardly of all. Perhaps I did it to reprise the educators whom the Khmer Rouge killed. Perhaps I did it to honor my great aunt, one of the top educators in the country, Saorin, known as Madame Tet Morm, Docteur Aggrege, professor at the school of medicine. Her picture was displayed in the Toul Sleng Museum in Cambodia. She and many other professionals were tricked into returning from France to assist with the rebuilding of the country, as announced by the Khmer Rouge. They did not anticipate that their own citizens would kill them.

Furthermore, the objective of this book is to facilitate healing and reconciliation for myself and, ideally, for others who share similar experiences.

I hope to encourage other survivors to tell their stories because their voices add to the history of Cambodia during the Khmer Rouge era. I also wish that the Khmer Rouge supporters would add to the story of how they believed that their behaviors would lead to restoring the country back to greatness once more.

Overall, I am satisfied with how I live my life. The emotional scar reminded me of the past, but I never allowed the past to define me. I used the past to find purpose in life, for I knew I was lucky to survive the Khmer Rouge.

I only hope that survivors like me use the past to find a greater purpose in life instead of trying to hide the past because of shame and guilt. I have learned that things that were kept hidden would not last. It came out in despair and viewed the world with a limited conscience. I hope that by understanding and accepting the past, we all can come to terms with historical trauma; otherwise, we will not stop pointing fingers at innocent people for making our lives miserable.

Lastly, I am thankful for my maternal grandmother, Mak Yay, Lavorn Ven. She had a dream of learning. She got her wishes through her children and grandchildren. She was able to see a new world in America, although she was illiterate in her native language. She waited for eight years to see the rest of her family reunited in America. It was her vision of learning that gave me the strength to pursue higher education, as I was determined to know more about my past. I hope that my father, brothers, grandparents, aunts, and uncle, who perished during the Khmer Rouge, did not die in vain. Their spirits will live for many generations to come.

Chapter Eight
Restoring Sense of Self

*"Without memory, there is no healing. Without forgiveness,
there is no future."*

--Desmond Tutu

Forgiveness

A 1984 Nobel Peace Prize winner and an Archbishop,
Desmond Tutu was a wise man. In his book, "No Future
Without Forgiveness," he defined forgiveness as
"abandoning your right to pay back the perpetrator." At the
same time, he insisted that we had to remember to seek
healing and forgiveness.

As much as I hated thinking about the past, I knew I
couldn't ignore the painful memories of living through the
Khmer Rouge. If I chose to forget those times, it would feel
like I was also forgetting my father, brothers, grandparents,
uncles, and aunts. I held on to them even though the
memories of their last moment on earth tormented me. Just
because they did not survive, it did not mean that they never
existed. They were among the millions of people who
perished during the Khmer Rouge. I wondered about the
families who had no survivors. Who would remember them?
Who would speak on their behalf? Who would know if they
were the family who had been around for thousands of
years? Who could describe how kind and compassionate
their families were?

Archbishop Tutu was right. To forgive, one had to
remember. What I remember during the Khmer Rouge
regime was deceitful, hatred, cruelty, lack of compassion,

exploitation of the innocent and ignorance, the abuse of power, opportunism, lack of virtue, and the meltdown of a nation.

To me, it was scary to remember how deplorable human beings could be. Nevertheless, I have to remember so that I can forgive. In addition, I want to remember so that I can inspire others to share theirs. By sharing memories, I hope that perpetrators who remained silent and denied what they did were not for the good of the country, but it was wrong morally, ethically, and unacceptable.

Tutu added that forgiveness was not just for the victims but for perpetrators as well. I wish that those who inflicted harm on others intentionally and unintentionally would admit that what they were inspired to do to others was wrong. It was not good enough to admit in secret that it was justifiable, and it was not their fault, but the fault of the masterminds, the Khmer Rouge leaders, for those survivors who happened to be in the provinces where persecution for being city dwellers was less severe than in other areas. They should at least share their perspective as to why their families were spared when many were not. I wanted to know about all the people who had been through the Khmer Rouge, adults and children. When I read memoirs of survivors, I read about the worst encounters and the brutal behaviors of the Khmer Rouge members. However, I remembered that there was kindness among malice. For this reason, I am willing to forgive.

At the same time, I wondered what had happened to all of those perpetrators. I did not mean just the Khmer Rouge leaders who were brought to justice by the international court. I meant the ordinary people who felt the need to get retribution from innocent people who they perceived to be the enemies. What led them to believe that all city dwellers were corrupted? What they did was undoing the dream of my grandmother in hoping that even a small-town girl deserved to be educated.

I wondered what happened to the Khmer Rouge children who bullied me and pushed me off the riverbank onto many small trees with branches that could have stabbed me in the chest as I rolled down to the water. My life could have ended back then, but it did not. I could not help but wonder if they ever felt remorse for their actions. Or did they believe that I deserved to be treated with malice just because I was born in the city of Phnom Penh? They did not know that I came from a working-class family. The act of violence toward me was unwarranted. It was pure hatred. It was like Breaking Bad in the countryside.

Yet, I forgave their ignorance. I only hope that wherever they are, they can find internal peace, instead of hatred.

In addition, I wanted to forgive the woman who stole Mom's cup of rice to save Baron. It was the last resort that Mom risked using her only memorabilia from Dad, a wedding ring that she had sewn inside her bra for safekeeping. She kept it to get by each day. She kept it to remind herself that she was fortunate to have love, even though it was taken away from her in the most cruel way. The Khmer Rouge took everything from her one by one. Mom placed her trust in the woman she worked with for years. If she knew the underground trading, she knew somebody higher up, at least someone who would protect her, whereas Mom had no one to defend her if the deal went wrong. Mom knew the risk. She took it anyway to save her son's life. She could not watch another son die helplessly from starvation.

A diamond ring for a cup of rice. I wondered about the opportunists who had been collecting jewelry from the victims. How would they live their lives? Did they have remorse or guilt? Perhaps not, sometimes, I heard the adults confirm the obvious, that to live one had to cheat, lie, and take any opportunity given, it was the way of the world. I felt morally repugnant.

Unfortunately, Mom did not get her wishes. The woman claimed that her cup of rice was confiscated. In a way, Mom was lucky she didn't reveal where the rice came from. The woman acted like she was doing Mom a favor by not giving her the rice to help save her child. That night, Mom and I felt speechless, helpless, hopeless, and deeply hurt inside, but we did our best to comfort Baron. We wished that he would pull through with just a drop of water to keep his lip from being so dry. Mom said that her gut feelings told her that the woman took advantage of her situation and ate the rice herself. The woman knew Mom was desperate to save her son. Yet, there was no compassion and understanding of the importance of a child's life.

When Baron died, I hated the woman. I detested the selfish behaviors of adults. I believe I lost my trust in adults from that moment on. I knew many adults contributed to the pains and sufferings of others. Through my understanding of the causation, I forgave them for their foolishness to think that it was possible to make Cambodia great again. I forgave them for their lack of insight. At the same time, I wondered what kind of people they became. Would they use the rest of their lives doing good for others so that they could repent? Did they ask for forgiveness for the deaths because they had contributed to their demise? I would at least hope that they became better people because of the past.

Forgiven, I had. I even abandoned my right to pay back my perpetrators. I had no thoughts of revenge. After all, the perpetrators, in my view, failed to understand the big picture. They acted on fear of annihilation.

The only concern I had about the perpetrators was that did they felt remorse. Did they comprehend the ethical and moral implications of their actions during the Khmer Rouge regime? Did they begin to repent?

Moreover, I even forgave my paternal grandmother, Vanna, for the way she treated me during the Khmer Rouge. I did not know about her prejudice towards my mom. I knew that she was a woman who used her status as a mother to control her son. I understood that in her generation, it was considered "honorable" to listen to parents. Fortunately, Father was not obliged to take his mother's advice regarding his own well-being. When it came to a matter of the heart he would not trade his love for mom. He remained respectful to his mother, but not to her wishes. Unfortunately, Grandmother Vanna did not acknowledge Mom. She blamed Mom for bewitching her son. Perhaps, her justification due to the limited educational attainment she possessed. Or perhaps, she held on to her right as a mother to control her son. Apparently, she did not see in the best interest for her son. Instead, she approached life by prioritizing external values. Why do parents often assume that they make decisions in the best interest of their children without asking them about their hopes and dreams from an early age, so they could guide them towards those aspirations? Grandmother held on to her beliefs because she did not have strong values in the first place. I forgave her for treating me and my brother, Baron, badly for months during the Khmer Rouge. I only hoped that before she passed, she realized that the Khmer Rouge dismantled her entire family, and the resentment she had for Mom was irrelevant to the life-and-death situation that she was now in. In some way, I felt sorry for my paternal grandfather, Pol. I was told he once was about justice and righteousness. He was the most respected man in his town, where he enforced such strict rules to ensure peace and safety for everyone. Yet, he watched the Khmer Rouge and how they separated his children from their families in agony. He watched us surviving daily activities in disbelief at how his hard work boiled down to his grandchildren working in the field to contribute to Angka instead of an education. I could see the sadness in my grandfather's gentle face as he tried to stop the poison from spreading in my injury. I had been bitten while sleeping under the cottage, out in the open, by a creature that could have taken my life that night. I have forgiven him for not defending us against my grandmother. However, I knew he was declining in health, spirit, and the will to live. He was more concerned about our condition. He worried about his adult children. He felt helpless. At the same time, I was glad that I got to know him better during the Khmer Rouge. At least, I knew that he was a man of virtue and kindness.

Unfortunately, I did not get a chance to know my maternal grandfather, Ros Sok, well. Based on what I heard about him, he disappointed me. Certainly, he was born with some privilege. He should have done more to shape the society where he expected the best of his children. He did not do more to preserve the society and culture for his grandchildren. He suffered for abandoning integrity and morals to follow a society favoring selective groups. For this reason, I considered his actions self-centered. I tried to understand Ros Sok by the way he named his sons. His thoughts transformed significantly when he named his son. For instance, his eldest son was named Komsan. It meant leisure and happiness. It certainly reflected my uncle Komsan. He did not take things seriously. He has this leisurely smile about him. He is carefree yet dependable. Ros Sok named his second son Serei. It meant free. He was difficult to manage. He agonized over the Khmer Rouge's strict policy. He was not fit to live in a controlled environment. He was forced to marry and forced to consummation under the Khmer Rouge. To take his rights in that way was such cruelty to him. At least, when parents arrange a marriage as was the tradition, they do not force consummation, or it is a life and death situation should a person refuse. To Uncle Serei, the Khmer Rouge took more than freedom of choice away from him. The events during the Khmer Rouge affected his sense of purpose in life. The third son was named Veasna. It meant luck. He was indeed a lucky man. He told me how fortunate he was during the Khmer Rouge, as he was assigned the easiest job and had access to enough nutrition to support himself. As time passed during the nineteen-sixties, Ros Sok had more Western influence when he named his younger sons Lindy, Amara, and Amarong. As for the girls, he was more sentimental. He named Mom after his great-aunt, Saoran. He named his youngest daughter Dara. It meant star. Aunt Fany and Aunt Chanty were more like him in terms of personality. They were considered to have a short fuse. Mak Yay gave birth to thirteen children, but only ten survived past adulthood. I did not ask about the rest of the names.

I did not think highly of Ros Sok because he too took advantage of society that allowed men to engage in multiple affairs. It was the example set by the monarchy. Grandfather had a second wife with a different set of household and children. It was allowed in society. He had three other children. Mom said that she met the woman once. It was ironic no one knew her name.

Mak Yay accepted her fate. Instead of feeling sorry for herself she used her energy to focus on her children and religion. She remained composed by acknowledging that she had no influence over others' decisions, even when those decisions contradicted ethical principles. As a result, she gained great fortune by living in America and having her children alive.

Whereas Grandfather Ros Sok trapped in the Khmer Rouge regime. He died shortly in the province where his ancestry came from. I was told that he starved himself to death. He did it because he knew the Khmer Rouge would find out about his former occupation shortly. He would not give the satisfaction to the Khmer Rouge for terminating him for meeting the target group to be persecuted. He rather did it willingly. It was his way.

But why? Was he afraid of the punishment? Did he regret parting with Mak Yay? Or perhaps, he realized that he contributed to the toxic society where selfishness overshadowed kindness and compassion.

After he died, his second wife and three younger children were taken away. They were not seen again. I wondered why he ended his life. Would he make the same choice if he knew that it would cause his family's lives? I wondered why he felt compelled to judge himself poorly. Why did he have a guilty conscience? Or perhaps, for someone like him, who spent almost half a century working to protect others and had a certain amount of influence on the law, felt that he did not do enough. Perhaps, he could not stand and watch the senseless brutality and savagery under the Khmer Rouge. At the same time, I thought of how selfish he was to think only of himself. I also thought he might have regretted and felt remorse toward Mak Yay, so he punished himself. More importantly, being an accomplished man, he should regret not doing more to protect his family and country.

I thought of the hypocritical society that believed in the sacredness of marriage, yet it was acceptable for men to commit infidelity. However, it was not the same for women. If a woman had an affair, she was demeaned to be less than a human. If a man had an affair, it was essential. The double standard existed years prior to the twentieth century. At least, Mom's generation made progress in the fact that women were allowed to learn.

At the same time, the class system created inequality in education, economics, and justice. Perhaps it was the reason that drove people to join the Khmer Rouge. It was the offered of equality by eliminating the class system. I wondered if the rural people knew about taking away the people's rights to live with dignity as well. The Khmer Rouge did not just confiscate all private properties, but also killed people under the name of corruption, or "the enemies of the state," by having prior knowledge of the influence of a democratic system. How could I forgive the Khmer Rouge leaders for their manipulation of innocent followers? How could I forgive the Khmer Rouge leaders for their twisted point of view? Their pursuit of notoriety was filled with paranoia and deception. In the end, it was not about returning Cambodia to the greatness of the Khmer Empire era; it was about destroying the core values of being the Khmer people like my Mak Yay. I can forgive them for my own sake, but I will not condone their behaviors. It was a sin to make uneducated people lead the educated group.

For example, during the Khmer Rouge regime, people who wore eyeglasses were considered intelligent and educated. Therefore, they were subject to elimination. If the Khmer Rouge members had knowledge about eyeglasses, they would understand that eyeglasses are used for improved vision.

The Khmer Rouge members who managed each camp and province were as brutal. They cultivated fears in us children as well. For example, my brother Varen suddenly had night blindness (Nyctalopia). The food we were allowed to eat was in the evening, after performing our daily assigned duties. As the daylight faded away, Varen could not see. He did not tell Mom, Dad, and me until he got lost one day, coming back to the shed. He frequently missed meals as he hurried to reach the shed before nightfall, where he allocated the tasks independently from me and my two younger brothers. Once he told us, Mom asked if he could appeal to his group leader to get his food ratio in advance. Right away, he refused. He was too proud. He would not use his disadvantage to gain any favor.

"No. I can manage." Even during the acrimonious time, Varin had his principles in tack. He would not accept compromise to make things easier for himself, that was, if he was given some leeway. He did not ask. He was determined to overcome the challenges.

Apparently, night blindness is a result of cataract issues and the lack of Vitamins. The minute the sun was about to set, Varen knew that he had to finish his meal quickly, so he walked back to our hut. Once I found out about his condition, I was mindful to finish my meal quickly so that I could guide him. There were no streetlights. Sometimes, it was the fireflies that lit the way for me. However, there were times when I could not get to him on time. He got lost a few times. Varen was determined not to let Mom and Dad worry about his condition on top of their concern over the situation we were in. I thought in a million years, I would never forgive and forget what the Khmer Rouge had done to my family. On the contrary, I found myself forgiving and admiring the maturity that my younger brothers displayed during adversity. I believed they would want me to forgive as well. I believed they kept my soul intact. While other survivors could only think of horrendous words to describe the Khmer Rouge members and supporters, I still believed that there was good among them as well, like Srey and her Mom, Mett Nang.

Acceptance

I could not forgive without accepting the fact that what had happened during the Khmer Rouge regime had shattered my human spirit. The thoughts of how my three brothers died gave me a sudden shortness of breath each time. However, I am determined never to forget such a senseless crime because I never wanted to forget my brothers.

There is no denying that I carry childhood trauma. I accept it as much as I accept the past. This way, I learn to recognize trauma symptoms. I learn to be mindful when I am sad, fearful, and angry. I wish not to be despairing, resentful, and numb just because I failed to accept my past traumatic experience. I hope to achieve inner peace. I can only do that if I accept myself.

It has been forty-nine years since the Khmer Rouge regime. I watched adult survivors decline in their mental, emotional, and physical health. The latest trend was early dementia. Twenty-five years ago, diabetes was a growing disease in the Cambodian community. It was trauma-related consumption.

Prior to the Khmer Rouge, there was a saying, "We eat to live." After the Khmer Rouge, "We live to eat." When we eat to live, we only consume enough to maintain nutrition for the body to function well. When we live to eat, we respond to our trauma; we tend to eat more than we should to make up for the time that we were deprived of eating to satisfy our wellness. This saying in the Cambodian community was the origin of the many diabetes patients among the Khmer people.

By understanding the symptoms of trauma and accepting the fact that I carried the trauma with me, I have become mindful when I eat. Food is also my coping mechanism. Sometimes, I feel that I need more than I should. Yet, I am aware of the impact if I continue to indulge my emotional and mental behavior. While I know my limit when it comes to food consumption, I find joy in seeing the abundance of food available. My favorite outing is going to the grocery store. I would stroll to each aisle and look at different types of food. The snack section captures my attention the most. My eyes lit up like a kid in a candy store. I felt that I was in a candy store. The variety of candies, cookies, crackers, chips, and bread took my breath away. Wow! If only I could eat. I would buy some snacks that were on sale. I might not eat it myself, but I save it when I have young relatives visiting, and then I watch them enjoying the snack. My sons would always inspect expiration dates prior to giving them to guests. They warned their younger cousins to cook snacks for a certain period in case of any food shortage; Mom would have plenty.

Nonetheless, the minute I reflected on myself, I could not help but feel mental exhaustion. It felt like I had been running a marathon all my life. Somehow, my body does not know how to respond to leisure. I felt more hallowed when my youngest left home to go to college. Suddenly, my body went into shock. For the first time, I had vertigo. It was a severe dizzy spell that I thought my head was going to fall off my body. Then, one day, I woke up to find that one side of my body was completely numb, froze, and unable to move. I began to feel pain on the right side of my body. The Dr. said it was a muscle spasm. I told myself it was a stroke and attempted to prepare mentally about how near my time would end. After all, I had anticipated death since the Khmer Rouge. I knew now it was part of my trauma, although I am not afraid of death. I thought of it often. However, I was afraid that I did not do enough for the time that I had. I felt that there was a reason I cheated death multiple times during the Khmer Rouge. I had to repent by doing good for others; perhaps I would make my father and brothers proud when I met them again in the afterlife.

Healthcare professionals only assumed that I experienced the stress of daily life like everyone else. I get anxiety medication whenever I have an episode. Mental health discussions would never be initiated unless I volunteered the information from my childhood background. I learned about phantom pains on my own through reading. I learned about how my mind tricked my body into reacting.

At least, I know that the price of surviving the Khmer Rouge is a lifetime of trauma. The heavy burden I felt on watching the act of atrocious cruelty toward young children stayed in my heart. It was no wonder that many survivors chose to forget about the past altogether. However, forcing oneself to erase the memories of the past led to a decline in mental and physical health. I saw many survivors who had early dementia. It was sad to witness that they even forgot about the children that they gave birth to in America. Sometimes, I felt that I might have dementia as well. I have noticed my short-term memories are declining. I could not remember the most recent memories, yet I remembered the scenes of the Khmer Rouge clearly. Perhaps I would rather store the memories of my father and brothers than the memories I accumulated over the years.

At least, I am aware of trauma. Sometimes, I could not control my brain from switching to survival mode. The experience taught me to be alert, prepared, and cautious. When I packed for a three-day event, I tended to pack like I was going for three months; even on a day trip, I packed food. I could not travel without food, even though I knew that I would stop buying more food on the road just because it was something different. The Khmer Rouge taught me well about the three-day evacuation. I would never accept that three days turned into three years and eight months. For some of us, it was four years before we could see the highway again. Professionals would call this part of my brain the limbic system. The limbic system helps control my emotions and behaviors. However, when I feel that there is a lack of trust in my environment, I go into overreaction mode. My brain gave me three ways to react: fight, flight, or freeze. I often either fled or shut down. Fighting took too much time and energy, so I usually chose to escape because starting over felt easier. Other times, I just stayed numb, telling myself the problem wasn't big enough to deal with. I deluded myself into thinking that it is better to choose the battle wisely to win the war than to engage in any small confrontations that waste unproductive energy.

Fortunately, I learned from my son how to deal with small things. If I deal immediately with the small issue that has arrived, I prevent it from becoming a bigger issue. This way, there would never be the huge catastrophe that I had seen in my culture. I admitted I came from a culture that avoids confronting problems. It was always about displaying the best behaviors regardless of internal harm. As a result, the suppressed feelings came out in an ugly way during the Khmer Rouge. It was not just the punishment against political opposition but classes, bias, and against social norms.

Even though I am living in America, the culture of obedience is embedded within me. Sometimes, I find it difficult to challenge the status quo. Therefore, my safe harbor was to flee and regroup when I felt injustice. In some way, I live in the past instead of allowing progress to take its course, like accepting the fact that it is healthy to solve small problems at a time. However, knowing that I carried a certain amount of trauma, I made every effort to question whether I applied common sense to the decision that I made for the improvement of quality of life, not just for myself but for later generations.

In addition, I was disappointed when I watched many adults within my family and community carry biased attitudes and behaviors toward Vietnamese people here in America. They even imposed their dislike on their children as to whom to love and marry. It was about the "historic enemy." It would never work. It would bring shame to the family if ethnic Vietnamese were among Cambodians. I wanted to understand why the hatred was so deep.

I grew up hearing all kinds of slang words used to de-scribe Vietnamese people who lived in Cambodia. When the act of violence occurred, it was said to be "Jole Yoon" (becoming Vietnamese). It described how violent Vietnam-ese people were. For years, I thought Cambodian people were discriminated against by the Vietnamese solely because of their invasion. In fact, according to David Chandler, there was a historical document by the Emperor of Vietnam to release Vietnamese prisoners into Cambodia for the sake of the Vietnamization of the people.

I could not imagine how the Khmer people survived all those years. They assumed that they did not deserve to learn from the best, but the misbehaviors of individuals who needed to correct their behaviors; instead, they were sent out to break bad on the innocent population who believed in doing "no harm" according to the Buddha's teachings. I wondered about the violence unleashed among the murderers, rapists, thieves, and swindlers. Was it the reason the Cambodian population became indignant about the ethnic Vietnamese?

I suddenly felt that there was some truth in what my aunt said about the Khmer Rouge. She said it was the Vietnamese who killed people. I saw the Khmer people who killed each other. She was determined to believe that the perpetrators were the Vietnamese whose for centuries wanted to exterminate the Khmer people so that they could absorb the land. This inherited hatred carried on for centuries even the melting pot of multi-ethnics existed in Cambodia.

For this reason, I wanted to prove to my family, who refused to acknowledge that ethnicity had nothing to do with crimes. It is the behaviors of individuals. In 2024, I utilized Ancestry.com to analyze my DNA. I was six percent Vietnamese. My point in doing so was to eliminate discrimination and bias among my family and community. If we all were to do DNA testing, I was sure that at least ninety percent of us would already have mixed with the DNA that was not desirable from the decision that was made hundreds of years ago. What remained true in our minds and souls was the fact that we chose good over bad to continue our lives.

When I accepted the past, I also accepted myself. I accepted that I lived through a horrible history in Cambodia. I also accepted the fact that I came from an ancestral background and am a descendant of the Khmer Empire era, which such sacred of unwavering wisdom.

At the same time, I accepted the broken society and how people became cynical. I never heard positive praise from the Cambodian people. My mother was unable to tell me the good that I achieved. She would tell others, but not to me directly. The concept of putting others before oneself led to self-destruction. We praised other ethnic accomplishment, but we failed to recognize our own and appreciated each other. This was the reason of polluted society. For centuries and generations, we were taught to be humble.

A frequently expressed remark by elders when observing children was:

"She looks so cute and charming. She must be Chinese or Vietnamese." Especially, if the girl had light skin. However, even if they knew the parents were both Cambodians, they still made such comment.

I found my culture to be oppressive. I wondered why we felt compelled to put ourselves down and lift others up. Did we lose what it was like to have self-worth? There was never a positive story I heard about the Khmer people, except when it was bad. Some people blamed themselves for losing the Khmer Empire. However, no one explained why. There had to be a reason. There was a story that made Khmer's later generations feel bad about each other.

It was said that long ago, during the first Siam invasion. Siam was today Thailand. The Siam Great Army could not penetrate the wall into the Khmer Empire's territory. Somehow, the empire was protected by a mystical jungle. The jungle became the fortress guarding the Khmer empire. The Siam army knew that it could only break from the inside.

Therefore, they threw gold coins into the forest. When ordinary people came across the shiny gold coins, they began to tell each other. Since knowing the value of the goal, coins, people rushed to get a piece of it. They unknowingly cut down ancient trees that had stood for thousands of years. Exposed, defenseless, and vulnerable, the Siam army succeeded in their invasion.

For the Khmer adults who told the story over and over again was to remind younger generations about the fault of the Khmer people. They described the self-destruction, but they never shared the root cause of why the people did what they did. Was it greed? Why continue to blame each other for the fall of the Khmer Empire? Why continue to believe that we were fewer than others because we allowed the Khmer Empire to disappear? Where were the leader, king, and advisors?

Aristotle warned us that inequality brought instability. The culture of absolute power to the king and his leaders led to such a catastrophe. Perhaps the leaders were so consumed with immediate gratification that they forgot to look out for others. Or, possibly, they failed to safeguard what they had achieved due to arrogance or complacency.

Instead of blaming each other for the need to collect the gold coins, the storytellers should have recognized the root cause of why people were willing to expose themselves to wealth. If cooperation and loyalty, as I was taught in "love thee neighbors and do no harm," there should not be a need for capitalism in the first place, right? But somehow, even though we were taught the quality of life was to live well with unyielding wisdom and inner peace, why did we hate each other so much that it came to the Khmer Rouge regime?

Looking back at Cambodia's history, I have to be in awe to call myself Cambodian. The King, Jayavarman II, inspired the people to build Angkor Wat. The architectural innovation at that time was stunning. It was built even before London and Paris were established.

French explorer Henri Mouhot discovered Angkor Wat in 1860. He was in disbelief. Some conspiracy theorists claim that Angkor Wat was built by people other than the Indigenous Khmer. Mouhot inquired with native speakers about the individuals and the type of people who built Angkor Wat. He recorded the words of the native who described the builders as "Giant."

Mouhot understood that the word "giant" was metaphorical. It referred to the spirit of the people who came together to build something for future generations to remember what they could accomplish together with grace and pride. Mouhot admitted that the temple of Angkor Wat displayed the genius, strength, and patience of its people. He also suggested that it was purposefully done to prove to future generations their strengths and brilliant minds.

At the same time, some historians suggested that Angkor Wat was built using slaves to do so. However, I did not see any evidence of such forced labor lasting for centuries. What I admired about Angkor Wat was the meticulous detail that was done because of the pride, patriotism, and cooperation of the people who came together to leave a legacy for their descendants. The carving on the stone wall suggests the love of work and the pride of the people. If it were forced labor, just like during the Khmer Rouge, people would not feel so displaced and exhausted mentally that they needed to scatter around the globe to find sanctuary from the horrific dehumanization of certain groups of people. I believe he was a great leader who inspired people to greatness. To me, Angkor Wat is the greatest place for the Khmer people to remember their ancestry.

Finally, I accepted that there was some truth to what my aunt and other survivors said about the Khmer Rouge.

"It was not the Khmer people. It was the Vietnamese people who were embedded within the Khmer community so that one day they could take the entire country." At first, I thought how absurd it was. Then, I realized that their statements were a reaction to the widespread settlement among the criminals of Vietnam as ordered by the emperor, who thought little about the well-being of innocent Khmer people.

To me, learning about my own history has reminded me of the inner strength and the unbreakable nature of our Khmer spirit.

Restoration

"No race can prosper till it learns that there is as much dignity in tilling a field as in writing a poem. It is at the bottom of life that we must begin and not at the top. Nor should we permit our grievances to overshadow our opportunities."

-- Booker Washington

Upon being liberated from slavery, an African American educational leader, Booker Washington, gave a profound warning to his community with the message above. He was right. After years of being dehumanized and existing only for the purpose of serving others and to be used to enhance the wealth of others, they had to learn how to understand that their lives were as important as those they served. They needed to realize that they had just as much dignity as the people they served. It was important to start from the bottom, not the top, so they could feel proud of themselves for accomplishing small tasks. It was about building character, learning the true meaning of value and self-worth. It was meant to cultivate human dignity after being used for the purpose of labor. It was learning to understand that they were as capable as those they served. It was about accepting that they, too, were the same human species as the people who forced them to perform many types of tasks and were made to believe that their worth was less than those they served. They had never been given a chance to be as capable as the people who bought them. Therefore, it was imperative to learn from the beginning.

Somehow, I feel that as a Cambodian and Khmer descendant, I should learn from the bottom like Booker Washington recommended for the African American community after slavery. It was not just after the Khmer Rouge that we needed to restore who we are as humans. It seemed like we had lost our spirits and souls long ago. Our minds and bodies were infected with toxins of immorality. We have been polluted and exploited for centuries. It was due to the autocratic leadership, colonizers, invaders, geopolitical influence from the West, and opportunists. The culture of obedience suppressed people from speaking up against injustice, inequity, and prejudice. Power and influence were used to oppress people. In addition, the social class system was designed to divide people and trigger hate among each group. The thousands of years of peace and cooperation with one another under the teaching of Buddha were now corrupted. Perhaps it began in the 1800s when Vietnam took control of Cambodia and attempted to Vietnamization of the Khmer population by releasing Vietnamese prisoners to break bad on the Khmer people. When I asked my elders why we held such grudge and resentment toward the Vietnamese ethnic, as much as not to allow the next generation to even marry Vietnamese ethnic, they answered as though they knew the improper conduct of the ethnic group by heart. The words they described to me were untrustworthy, deceptive, violent, unethical, promiscuous, undisciplined, and selfish. Their fears certainly justified the history found by David Chandler when he described that the Khmer people were not treated with respect when the Emperor of Vietnam released Vietnamese prisoners to live among the Khmer people. I could not imagine living among criminals who preyed the innocent people. It was startling when mom's cousin spoke of her childhood and why she was separated from her parents prior to the Khmer Rouge. She ended up in Battambang instead of the small town outside of Phnom Penh.

"My dad told me never to return home." She said.

"Why?" I asked.

She described the incident of a home robbery where she had to hide quietly for a while. Her parents were frantic, knowing that they had nothing valuable except for their teenage daughter. The robbers took off with the bike reluctantly. Her parents were sure that she was the target. The next day, her father shipped her off to live with relatives outside of her birthplace. She claimed that she contributed to the home invasion because she was spotted outside of the home. What kind of state at a time when a young woman could not even play outside or wander in nature? The environment was not conducive to growth anymore. It was interesting as she told the story; she even added that the perpetrators were Vietnamese. I could not help but press for evidence.

"How do you know?"

"I heard them speak Vietnamese." She confirmed. It was two guys.

Indeed, the Cambodian people feared the Vietnamese people. Apparently, they never overcame the fears of living under the control of Vietnam at one point and the spread of criminal acts on the other. Cambodians continued to warn their children of how dangerous it would be to co-exist with the Vietnamese ethnic. This belief continued to pass on to the next generations.

I found my answer to why the elders still had a strong objection to Vietnamese ethnicity. As for me, I enjoyed having many friends from different backgrounds, including Vietnamese. I never asked what ethnic makeup they were as long as they had the same characteristics as me. I felt more troubled for the elder generations that had never addressed their trauma than to add another trauma of the magnitude of genocide during the Khmer Rouge. I wondered about the impact centuries of trauma had on their spiritual, moral, ethical, emotional, and physical health. Even in today's reality, where we started our new homes in America, I still hear of the fear and paranoia relating to Vietnamese ethnicity. The stories I heard supported the historical context.

What was more important was the effort of restoration? How can we find reconciliation for ourselves and our community? As the archbishop Tutu recommended, we must forgive. It was the only way that we could restore what it was like to live in a world where we don't fear each other, where we helped one another, as I used to hear that Mak Yay would buy food for a pregnant woman standing by the beef skews stall to smell the taste when she could not afford to buy the meat. After giving her meat budget away, Mak Yay would alter her menu to only vegetables and fish because it was cheaper. I loved hearing stories of Mak Yay because it restored my faith in humanity. She represented the kindness and compassion that we all should have. However, we should also realize that the past left us with skepticism, despair, and resentment. It was up to us to learn how to renew our sense of worth. Only when we know our worth that we respect others' worth as well.

I determined to erase my skepticism and judgment of the Vietnamese ethnicity by looking within myself. For years, I heard that my paternal grandmother could speak Vietnamese. When I asked whether she was of Vietnamese descent, no one in my family admitted, "Yes." It was like they were ashamed of who she was. At the same time, when she displayed bad behavior, they did not hesitate to say that she was "Vietnamese" out of anger. I was curious whether my paternal grandmother was of Vietnamese ethnic or not within her DNA. So, I submitted my own DNA testing on Ancestry.com. Indeed, I have six percent of Vietnamese descendants. I used my six percent to point out who I am when family members suggested that Vietnamese was bad. They spoke out of trauma. They failed to see the current situation and how we evolved. I serve as a reminder to my family that I have the ethnic makeup that they feared, but if they know me, then they know that I was not at all what they had thought. The point is we ought to stop being paranoid.

Moreover, I wonder if the Khmer Rouge unleashed grievances onto the Vietnamese minority living in Cambodia because of the criminals' perceptions. At the same time, the French did bring in some Vietnamese population to work in the colonization government for almost a century. Cambodians had lost their point of view between good and bad with all the suppression of feelings and rights. For that reason, we need to restore our humanity, minds, hearts, and souls. After all, we had been demeaned, neglected, and abused for the purpose of maintaining superiority for certain groups of individuals.

Arran Stibbe put it best, "Words and actions are used to systematically lower the social status of one party in order to feed the other party's desire for superiority." What I have heard growing up was about putting down one group to gain the favor of the other group. It was the pollution of the mind. How was it possible for Chinese Cambodians to believe that they were better than the Indigenous Khmer people when their accumulation of wealth came from the country and the people who had thousands of years of history in it? How was it possible to have such an ego without compassion for the country that allowed you the opportunity to get ahead more so than the Indigenous people who were taught to have no greed and to be satisfied with a life of peace and inner wealth? The audacity to publicize a narrative that the Chinese were better than the Khmer was to demean and put down the Khmer people for their own egoism. Was it one of the reasons that the Khmer Rouge killed the ethnic Chinese minority? I only knew that we had lost our morals and ethics of what we held dear to our hearts in terms of "thou shall not harm" others including the verbal attack.

Fortunately, to begin again, I had Mom and Mak Yay, who stayed true to their beliefs. Mak Yay's kindness and compassion allowed me to restore human dignity. Mak Yay and Mom valued education and encouraged my pursuit of knowledge. They were able to see that problems could be solved if we were well-informed and learned critical thinking skills. The joys of reading, whether fiction or non-fiction, would set off an aspiration in me. I was lost during the Khmer Rouge, but I did not forget where I came from. With education, I was able to put the pieces of my broken spirit back together to some degree of normalcy.

Nevertheless, I assumed that by involving and working in the Cambodian community, I would find collective healing. Instead, I felt the burden of such trauma that it was tougher for collective bodies to see the process of healing through learning why we did what we did to each other. I saw many people use nostalgia to get by each day. I did the same thing sometimes. However, I did not want to waste all the time that we had in this life to make amends for what we saw went wrong in the past.

Granted, the majority of people who survived the Khmer Rouge were women and children. With many educators and skilled individuals killed, most of the remaining population were uneducated and failed to see the important aspect of rebuilding oneself through restoring the values that we lost.

Therefore, what kind of life do they see for themselves when they start over? What encouragement and guidance could they provide for their children? The only security that they had in mind was to do what their parents did to them. I watched many young teenage girls my age gets married for the sake of their parents. They did not even finish high school, even though there were only a few months left. It was even tougher for them to find peace and closure without realizing the opportunity to understand the background, as we started over as teenagers in a new country. I could only hope that they knew more than to enforce cultural beliefs onto their second-generation American-born. It was about restoring the dignity that Booker Washington saw in the possibility of greatness by beginning from the bottom.

Additionally, faith has restored many of the elder spirits. Many survivors, including my mother, used faith to live each day. Mak Yay used faith to ground herself during difficult times. For eight years, she held on to the belief that her children would be safe during the Khmer Rouge while she waited in the United States for news. Mom used faith to convince herself that her beloved husband and three sons ended their lives suffering and only met with nirvana. The growth in Buddhist temples all over the United States is due to such a need for the restoration of human spirits after the Khmer Rouge. Using faith to relieve all worry, sadness, and guilt was what had helped many people in the community.

In addition to faith, I hope that we are more aware of our own subconscious reactions to issues that are affecting our daily lives. Sometimes, we overuse nostalgia to numb ourselves. We need to understand our behaviors so that we protect ourselves from being vulnerable to prey. Booker was right when he suggested that we need to begin at the bottom; only then will we know our worth. We need to rebuild our immune system. Inner strength and security protect us from external nonsense. When we know our worth, we make conscious decisions. We drown out misinformation and those who took advantage of our emotions and feelings. Recognizing and accepting our past helps us regain our dignity and makes us stronger. Whenever I faced challenges as an adult, I reminded myself that I had survived the Khmer Rouge. Compared to that, other problems felt small. That mindset gave me the strength to reach many of my goals.

Lastly, I believe humor contributed to my sense of self. I found joy in laughter. Laughing took away every sadness I might have had in the past. There were many misinterpretations of our new language and culture. Being surrounded by family members had helped me to forget about my painful childhood.

Assimilating into a new environment, culture, and language took time. I learned along with younger children. For many adults, misinterpreting words and actions were common.

One memorable moment about growing up in America was a misinterpretation. For example, my aunt, Chanty, misinterpreted the action most hilariously. It was the day that she had nieces, her own children, and me in the car. I believed we had come from the beach that day. There were five children. She and I were the only adults. I was about nineteen at the time. She drove a Ford Windstar minivan. As she exited the freeway, there was a car that cut right in front of us without signaling and leaving enough space. She had to break frantically. She was scared and furious. The guy who thought he would go faster than she had to stop at the next stoplight. Aunt Chanty moved to the next lane and stopped at the same light. She wanted to tell the guy how she was feeling.

"I'm going to give that guy a finger." She announced, knowing that she would come to a complete stop next to him. She looked at the guy and flipped her finger.

I was busy looking at the guy's face for a reaction when I heard.

"Wrong finger, Mom!" her five-year-old son shouted in disappointment. My aunt had her thumb up confidently. I saw the confused expression on the other driver. He was uncertain how to respond to a thumb-up, though he anticipated some form of retribution for his earlier actions that frightened everyone if Aunt Chanty hadn't stopped in time. Then, the light turned green. She proceeded quietly for a second before we all burst into laughter. We could not stop laughing until tears were in our eyes. It was the best day of my life. When life and learning got tough, I thought of all the laughter we shared. Keeping humor alive was the best way to combat negative thoughts about the world and the people in it. I admired the Cambodian people for maintaining their humorous attitudes during the worst event in their lives, like pausing a moment to crack a smile when someone took the picture. Was it the culture? Perhaps it was the propriety we learned from a young age to appreciate every situation, even if it was not conducive to our souls. I have noticed that I tend to smile or laugh slightly when I feel uncomfortable during a conversation. Anyhow, I just knew that I had inherited the spirit of humanity through the ability to find joy in pain. I guess laughter is the painkiller of life.

Chapter Nine
Conclusion

Despite my traumatic childhood, I still believe in humanity and find joy in life by seeing the best in people. However, the past reminds me to stay resilient and persevere. Although the term "resilience" is frequently used to describe survivors, I am mindful of its meaning. The fact is, I was trained to be resilience. The Khmer Rouge converted me into a tolerance body where I could endure hardship. I was taught to suppress emotions, hunger, pains, and personal rights. As a result, I survived. Therefore, any subsequent challenges in life seem insignificant.

Alternatively, if I think my resilience stems from experience, I might see the world differently. I might believe that to be strong one had to endure hardship. This belief carried for generations. Mom used to mention an instance when her father disciplined her for playing instead of reading during her free time. Did grandfather believe that to make his children sturdy and tough was to have them endured pain? Mission accomplished. Mom is an expert in enduring pain and hardship.

If resiliency comes from endurance than I might lose the ability to be empathetic. I might assume that everyone would have the ability to overcome any challenges just like me. I might not see the severity of others' emotional and mental challenges. I might think of a "one size fit all" approach to reasoning. If it works for me than it should work for others as well. I might have the audacity to believe that if there is the next genocide I would survive it to. How ironic would that be? I thought about my ability to withstand hardship instead of how to prevent it. Subsequently, future generations would blame me for not doing my part to prevent history from repeating itself. I thought hard about the word resilience and how it would define me.

To me, true resilience is knowing where I came from and where I am going. The ability to distinguish between right and wrong is resilience. The courage to speak the truth is resilience. The ability to learn from the past is resilience. The courage to admit that one is wrong when one is making a mistake is resilience. I can only accept that I am resilient when I speak on behalf of those that are unable to speak for themselves. Finally, I can accept that I am resilient when I remind myself about the past so that I can change the future.

Granted, it was not easy to reflect on the past, especially the painful moment. Nevertheless, it is crucial to understand why people did what they did to others. For me, it is easier to forgive when I understand the causes.

I admitted that writing this memoir took a toll on my emotional, mental, and physical health. It was exhausting to recall the memories of injustice, inhumane, and imprisonment. More importantly, the memories of being repressed of thoughts, intelligence, emotions, behaviors, and food deprivation were enough to make me want to be mute, numb, dumb, and blind. If I am numb I would feel nothing. I would not feel such a burden for being a survivor. I would not have to ask, "what I could do for those who did not survive" (Frankle). Perhaps, I would be exactly like what the mastermind of the Khmer Rouge wanted me to be; mute, numb, dumb, and blind so that I would not question why, allowing the act of genocide to become normal when there is conflict. Therefore, I refused to forfeit my memories because it was too hard for me to bear, or it was too shameful for me to admit that I once lived through such a catastrophe that no children ever should endure.

As I remembered childhood trauma, I became more aware and mindful of my own behaviors. I learned to forgive myself for my shortcomings and others for their misled actions. If I did not accept my past, I would live in fear and resentment, despising the rules of law. After all, the law did not protect me when I was a child. Trust was probably the hardest to achieve because I would always have trust with reservation. At the same time, my worldview would be limited and distorted. I would make decisions based on feelings instead of what was right and wrong. I would be easily persuaded by power and the illusion of righteousness. I would measure my sense of worth based on what society perceived as valuable. I would easily give in to self-indulgent thinking that after a near-death experience, I deserved to live freely without consequences. I would live defensively, fearing it might be taken away by those who seemed to have it easier life than I had. I would react to every challenging situation without thinking of the roots of my sensitivity. I would be in cruise control of hypervigilance. I would live the rest of my life airing out grievances to the world. Those were the mental and emotional impacts of my childhood trauma if I did not recognize its existence.

Despite experiencing those symptoms, I continue to count my blessings. It was not by accident that I got to live when many others did not. It was not by accident that I reunited with Mak Yay in America. What had restored my human spirit was being around gentle and kindness.

On the other hand, I could not imagine if I failed to accept the past. I would have allowed trauma to consume me. If that were the case, what would my father and brothers think? Would they be disappointed?

Mom believed that their spirits guided us to safety. They performed miracles to protect us, even in the face of execution. There were countless times when Mom or I met dangerous circumstances. Yet, we still persisted. We are still alive. How could I ever let them down for not acknowledging who they were if my existence were because of them? I would be ashamed of myself if I became self-absorbed.

In fact, I was afraid to close my eyes because their images began to fade away from my memories. I have no picture of Baron and Phirum. However, I have a picture of Varen from my aunt's family collection. I do not want to forget how sensible and innocent they were. Regardless of their images, I will never let them die in vain. I knew if they had the opportunity to live like me, they would speak up for children who were abused unjustly during any kind of state conflict. They would ensure that no children should ever be caught in the crossfire of power between adults. I knew if they had a chance to survive, their lives would be filled of special moments. At the same time, my father and brothers would prefer that I lead a life with less grief and more hope. They would want me to live with dignity and pride. They would want me to enjoy the diverse cultures. Every time I went to the buffet, I thought of them. My eyes were bigger than my stomach at the site of the buffet stations offering the cultural cuisines in taste. I would jump at the opportunity to have a bit of everything. Yet, there was a tiny guilt that I wished my brothers would live to know that in America, we have a buffet.

Moreover, numerous Cambodian survivors dedicated their lives to supporting others. Perhaps, the guilt of living after what they had seen was too great not to be helpful to others. Or perhaps, it was a method for addressing their historical trauma. For this reason, I am proud to be Cambodian American.

Additionally, education is often considered a remedy. It assists me in confronting my past. I was able to come to terms with historical trauma by understanding the causes and the consequences. With understanding of the past, I was able to forgive the people of the past. The culture of submission and repression of feelings led to tension over time. It was extreme endurance and tolerance for centuries. The result of that endurance and tolerance was deadly.

Chandler (1996) admitted that the culture of obedience and hierarchy made it possible for exploitation. He stated that "the Cambodians had been victimized by five countries: Thailand, Vietnam (twice), France, the United States, and China." The exploitation took place over one hundred fifty years. I could not help but feel sympathetic to the people of the past. They tolerated injustice for centuries. They suffered mental anguish for generations. They were told to tolerate and endure because they had no choices. Their leaders failed them again and again. They had no access to education. They had no support for upward mobility. They could not change the status of their families without connection. When the Khmer Rouge offered a new solution, they accepted it out of desperation. As a result, they added more victims to the victimized society.

Regardless of our past victimization, we should not allow our grievances to overshadow our opportunities, as Booker Washington had suggested. We should show later generations what kind of people we are after being brutalized in so many ways. After all, we are the descendants of Khmer Angkor. We should be proud of the legacy they left for us to admire and inspire. Our enduring strength is a testament to our greatness.

I no longer despise Saloth Sar for tainting the last name Pol, for I believe he grew up without having a steady foot on the ground. He failed to understand human compassion. He deceived many people to believe that what he did was for them. The needs to return to the past was an illusion.

Finally, I hope that my story will encourage others to share their stories. I also hope that my story eases the pain we carry in our hearts. Understanding the past can help facilitate reconciliation within the community and family. It is imperative to learn from the past, no matter how uncomfortable it is.

Acknowledgements

I am fortunate to have a courageous mother who taught me not to give up on life and to find reasons to give back to society. Not only did she give me life, but she saved my life multiple times during the Khmer Rouge and led me to this better life in America.

I am grateful to my husband for keeping me grounded to achieve my goals.

I am proud of my sons, Ian and Baron, for their support and understanding.

Lastly, I am fortunate to have great family and friends who provide emotional, mental, and moral support.

In addition, I want to thank the following individuals for taking their valuable time to review the manuscript: Judy Green, Huntyce Moore, James Sanders, Diedre Wood, and Karin Stahl.

I would also like to thank Sayon Syprasoeuth for designing the cover page.

References

Bit, S. (1991). *The Warrior Heritage: A Psychological Perspective of Cambodian Trauma.* Seanglim Bit, El Cerrito, California.

Boss, P., & Carnes, D. (2012). The myth of closure. *Family Process, 51*(4), 456–469.

Brinkley, J. (2011). Cambodia's Curse: The modern history of a trouble land. Public Affairs.

Brown, K. M. (2004). Leadership for social justice and equity: Weaving a transformative framework and pedagogy. *Educational Administration Quarterly, 40*(1), 77–108

Chandler, D. P. (1991). *The tragedy of Cambodian history: Politics, war, and revolution since 1945.* New Haven, CT: Yale University Press.

Chandler, D.P. (2008). *A History of Cambodia.* Fourth Edition. Westview Press.

Hass, M. (2012). *Modern Cambodia's emergence from the killing fields: What happened in the critical years?* Los Angeles, CA. Publishing House for Scholars.

Kamm, H. (1998). Cambodia: Report from a Stricken Land. Arcade Publishing Inc. New York

Kiernan, B. (1996). *The Pol Pot regime: Race, power, and genocide in Cambodia under the Khmer Rouge, 1975-1979.* New Heaven, CT: Yale University Press.

Kiernan, B. (2004). *How Pol Pot came to power: Colonialism, Nationalism, and Communism in*

Cambodia, 1930-1975. New Haven & London. Yale University Press.

Pol-La Tour, S., & Kirkbribe, V. (2001). *Vantha's whisper*. Bloomington IN: Xlibris.

Schlund-Vials, C. J. (2012). *War, genocide, and justice: Cambodian American memory work*. Minneapolis: University of Minnesota Press.

Vickery, M. (1984). *Cambodia: 1975-1982*. Silkworm Books. O.S. Printing House, Bangkok.

Yang, K. (2003). Southeast Asian American children: Not the "model minority." *The Future of Children-Growing Up American*, *14*(2), 127–133.

Yathay, P. (1987). *Stay alive, my son*. New York. NY: The Free Press.

www.ingramcontent.com/pod-product-compliance
Lightning Source LLC
Chambersburg PA
CBHW071723120626
46550CB00001B/361